AL-FĀRĀBĪ AND HIS SCHOOL

Al-Fārābī and His School examines one of the most exciting and dynamic periods in the development of medieval Islam, that period which ran from the late ninth century to the early eleventh century AD. The Age is examined through the thought of five of its principal thinkers and labelled after the first and greatest of these, the Age of Fārābism.

It is demonstrated in this book that the great Islamic philosopher al-Fārābī, called 'the Second Master' after Aristotle, produced a recognizable school of thought in which others pursued and developed some of his own intellectual preoccupations. This school of thought, which Ian Richard Netton calls the 'School of al-Fārābī', was influenced by the thought of Plato, Aristotle and Plotinus, but it was much more than a mere clone of Greek thought – though one cannot ignore in all its work the profound Greek intellectual influence. Its adherents, including Yaḥyā b. ʿAdī, Abū Sulaymān al-Sijistānī, al-ʿĀmirī and Abū Ḥayyān al-Tawḥīdī, are described and assessed in this volume. Their thought is treated in *Al-Fārābī and His School* with particular reference to the most basic questions which can be asked in the theory of knowledge or epistemology. The book thus fills a lacuna in the literature by using this approach to highlight the intellectual continuity which was maintained in an age of flux. Particular attention is paid to the ethical dimensions of knowledge.

Ian Richard Netton, who is a leading authority in the field of Islamic philosophy and theology, has written a book which will appeal to all Arabists and Islamicists and students of philosophy, theology and ethics. He is Reader in Arab and Islamic Civilization and Thought at the University of Exeter. Among his many other publications is *Allāh Transcendent: Studies in the Structure and Semiotics of Islamic Philosophy, Theology and Cosmology*, also published by Routledge.

ARABIC THOUGHT AND CULTURE

This series is designed to provide straightforward introductions for the western reader to some of the major figures and movements of Arabic thought. Philosophers, historians, and geographers are all seminal figures in the history of thought, and some names, such as Averroes and Avicenna, are already part of the western tradition. Mathematicians, linguistic theorists, and astronomers have as significant a part to play as groups of thinkers such as the Illuminationists. With the growing importance of the Arab world on the international scene, these succinct and authoritative works will be welcomed not only by teachers and students of Arab history and of philosophy, but by journalists, travellers, teachers of EFL, and businessmen – in fact any who have to come to an understanding of this non-western culture in the course of their daily work.

Also available in this series:

IBN KHALDUN *Aziz Al-Azmeh*
IBN RUSHD (AVERROES) Dominique Urvoy
MOSES MAIMONIDES Oliver Leaman
THE ARABIC LINGUISTIC TRADITION
G. Bohas, J.-P. Guillaume, D.E. Kouloughi

Forthcoming:

IBN ARABI *Ron Nettler*
NAGUIB MAHFOUZ *Rasheed El-Enany*
AVICENNA *Lenn E. Goodman*
THE CLASSICAL HERITAGE IN ISLAM *Franz Rosenthal*

AL-FĀRĀBĪ AND HIS SCHOOL

Ian Richard Netton

ROUTLEDGE

London and New York

First published 1992
by Routledge
11 New Fetter Lane, London EC4P 4EE

Simultaneously published in the USA and Canada
by Routledge
a division of Routledge, Chapman and Hall Inc.
29 West 35th Street, New York, NY 10001

Material reprinted from *The History of al-Ṭabarī: Vol. XXX The ʿAbbāsid Caliphate in Equilibrium*, (SUNY, 1989) by C.E. Bosworth appears by permission of the State University of New York Press, © 1989 State University of New York. Material reprinted from *Philosophy of the Middle Ages*, Hyman and Walsh (eds), Hackett Publishing Company, Inc., 1987, Indianapolis, IN and Cambridge, MA appears with the permission of the publisher.

Typeset in 10 on 12 point Bembo by
Leaper & Gard Ltd, Bristol, England
Printed in Great Britain by
Clays Ltd, St. Ives plc

British Library Cataloguing in Publication Data
Netton, Ian Richard
Al-Fārābī and his school. – (Arabic thought and
culture; 5)
I. Title
181.07

Library of Congress Cataloging in Publication Data
Netton, Ian Richard.
Al-Fārābī and his school / Ian Richard Netton.
p. cm.
Includes bibliographical references and index.
1. Fārābī—Contributions in theory of knowledge. 2. Knowledge,
Theory of (Islam) I. Title.
B745.K53N48 1992
181′.6—dc20 91-42233

ISBN 0-415-03594-5 ISBN 0-415-03595-3 (pbk)

For my mother
Olive Christine Netton
with much love

And say: 'My Lord, increase me in knowledge'.

Qur'ān 20: 114

Knowledge is infinite since it originates from and ends in God, who is the Absolute Knower. Since knowledge is an aspect of divinity, seeking it, expanding and teaching it are considered important acts of divine worship.

Wan Mohd Nor Wan Daud,
The Concept of Knowledge in Islam

CONTENTS

FIGURES

PREFACE AND ACKNOWLEDGEMENTS

As the title indicates, this book deals with the thought of that great Islamic philosopher, al-Fārābī, and that of some of his disciples. However, in an attempt to bring out the real significance and importance of these thinkers, they have been viewed through what might be termed a specifically 'epistemological lens'. It is hoped that the freshness of this approach will both illuminate many areas of their thought – not just in the area of theory of knowledge – and indicate directions for future research. The Prophet Muḥammad, in a well-known tradition, bade his followers seek knowledge even as far as China. The habit of travel in search of knowledge and learning became well established in medieval Islam. This book therefore examines the thought of five major medieval thinkers by concentrating specifically on the area of epistemology. It must be stressed, however, that my book is not intended to be an *advanced* textbook of Islamic epistemology. Rather, it is a primer which asks, and concentrates upon, the most basic questions which may be asked in this field.

I would like to acknowledge permission given by Hackett Publishing Company, Inc., to reproduce material from *Philosophy of the Middle Ages*, ed. Hyman and Walsh, Hackett Publishing Company, Inc., 1987, Indianapolis, IN and Cambridge, MA. I am also grateful to the Hakluyt Society for permission to quote from H.A.R. Gibb, *The Travels of Ibn Baṭṭūṭa A.D. 1325–1354*, vol. 3, trans. H.A.R. Gibb, (Cambridge University Press for the Hakluyt Society, 1971); and to Cambridge University Press for permission to quote from A.J. Arberry, *Poems of al-Mutanabbī*, (Cambridge University Press, 1967). And I acknowledge here with gratitude a particular debt to three of my fellow scholars: Franz Rosenthal, Joel L. Kraemer and Majid Fakhry. My use of their works is acknowledged in my endnotes and reiterated in the Bibliographical Guide at the end of this volume.

I also thank the following, whose help has proved invaluable in the completion of this volume: Dr Christopher Gill, Senior Lecturer in Classics at the University of Exeter, who gave much-needed help in the understanding of Greek technical terminology; Mrs Sheila Westcott, Secretary of the Department of Arabic and Islamic Studies, University of Exeter, who typed parts of the manuscript of this book with her customary patience, efficiency and good humour; and Miss Heather Eva, Director of Exeter University's excellent Inter-Library Loans Department. I am deeply grateful to my copy-editor Sandra Jones and to my desk editor at Routledge, Jill Rawnsley, for the professional and caring way in which they have prepared for publication what was a very difficult typescript.

My final thanks and love, as always, go to my wife and family who patiently suffered the vagaries of an author trying to complete three books at the same time. I am pleased to say that this is one of them.

October 1991

Ian Richard Netton
Reader in Arab and Islamic Civilization and Thought,
University of Exeter

ABBREVIATIONS

d.	died
EI^2	Second Edition of *The Encyclopaedia of Islam*
EI^2 *Supp.*	Supplement to the above
reg.	*regnabat*
sér.	série
s.v.	*sub verbo*
t.	tome

1

THE AGE OF FĀRĀBISM

The Second Master and His Students

The Age of al-Fārābī – the 'Second Master' after Aristotle[1] – and of those who followed and developed his teachings was one of the richest intellectually in the entire development of medieval Islamic thought. The age will be characterized here in this book as the *Age of Fārābism*: it will be defined as running from the birth of al-Fārābī in AD 870 to the death of Abū Ḥayyān al-Tawḥīdī in about AD 1023. The very useful term 'Fārābism' itself, borrowed from and modelled on the usage of Ibrahim Madkour,[2] is designed to signal a philosophical current, worthy of respect *in its own right*, which is not to be considered as a mere facsimile of ancient Greek thought. The historical parameters AD 870–1023 provide a neat, if artificial, framework and structure within which to examine the phenomenon of Fārābism, enclosing as they do four other major thinkers, apart from al-Fārābī himself, who in one way or another interacted with, or were profoundly influenced by, the thought of the Second Master. These thinkers were: (1) Yaḥyā b. ʿAdī (AD 893/4–974); (2) Abū Sulaymān al-Sijistānī (d. *c.* AD 987/8); (3) Abū 'l-Ḥasan al-ʿĀmirī (d. AD 992); and (4) Abū Ḥayyān al-Tawḥīdī (d. *c.* AD 1023). It is the analysis of the thought and ideas of these four, together with those of al-Fārābī (AD 870–950) – an intellectual current designated globally in this book as 'Fārābism' – which constitutes the matter of what is presented here. Particular attention will be paid throughout to the epistemologies espoused by the above-named thinkers.

This is perhaps a suitable point to note, however, that the thought of Ibn Sīnā (AD 979–1037), the most distinguished philosopher of all both in the east and the west to be influenced by al-Fārābī,[3] is *not* treated within the compass of this book. He has been treated in many places at considerable length elsewhere.[4] Furthermore, the four thinkers discussed here as members of what is being described as the 'School of Fārābī', or adherents of Fārābism, are a representative selection only: it is not my contention that these four were the *only* followers of al-Fārābī.

The Age of Fārābism was one which encompassed major developments on both the political and religious fronts: it was certainly an age of deep instability and change. The few brief examples that follow must serve to illustrate this primary and elemental fact. It is only stressed here because it was the disruptive backdrop against which the thinkers discussed in this work lived, taught, wrote, thought and died: the fabric of their thought – not to mention their lives – could not help but be scarred, or even invaded, by these twin motifs of instability and change.

At the beginning of the tenth century AD the movement of the Qarāmiṭa, proponents of a complex theology akin to Ismāʿīlism, gained momentum: in AD 930 Mecca was attacked, many pilgrims were killed and the Black Stone set in the Kaʿba was carried off. The Qarāmiṭa later returned it in AD 951. Though their action was probably directed more at the commercial ramifications of the pilgrimage to Mecca than the pilgrimage itself,[5] the attack was devastating in its symbolism, striking as it did at a literal cornerstone of Islamic ritual. It may be said to constitute a valid and startling paradigm for the instability and change which beset the entire Age of Fārābism.

Other 'signs of the times' in that age are not difficult to discover: earlier the Būyids, who were influenced by, and tolerant towards, Twelver Shīʿism, Zaydism and Muʿtazilism, had assumed effective control in Baghdad in AD 945. During the tenth century AD the star of the Shīʿite Ḥamdānids rose and waned in Mosul and Aleppo. By contrast, that of the Ismāʿīlī Fāṭimids rose and became even stronger: Ismāʿīlī Islam achieved a political apotheosis with the capture of Egypt in AD 969 by the army sent by the fourth Fāṭimid Caliph, al-Muʿizz (*reg.* AD 953–75).

It is no accident than Shīʿism, with its alternative and thus frequently divisive interpretation of early Islam, should figure prominently in the few brief examples cited above. If, as one author maintains, the eighth and early ninth centuries AD were 'a period of revolutionary incubation'[6] for the Ismāʿīlīs, and indeed others, then the tenth century AD, which comprises the major part of the Age of Fārābism, may surely be accounted a period of revolutionary Shīʿite

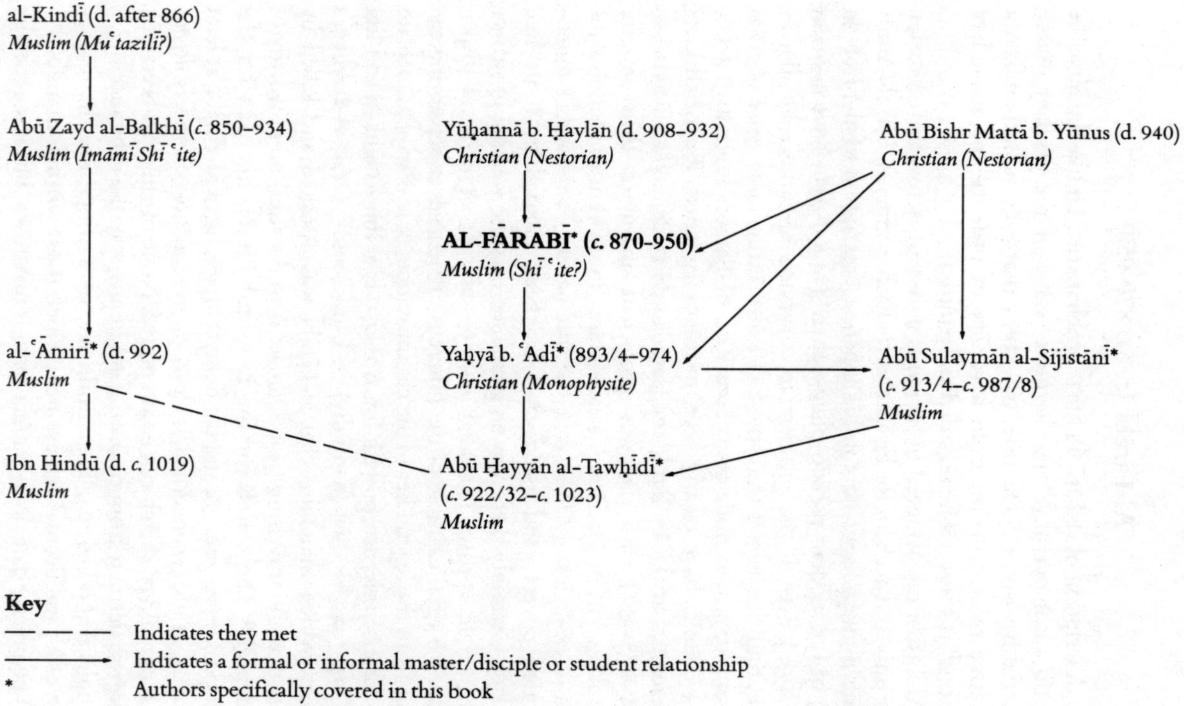
al-Kindī (d. after 866)
Muslim (Muʿtazilī?)
Abū Zayd al-Balkhī (c. 850–934)
Muslim (Imāmī Shīʿite)
Yūḥannā b. Ḥaylān (d. 908–932)
Christian (Nestorian)
Abū Bishr Mattā b. Yūnus (d. 940)
Christian (Nestorian)
AL-FĀRĀBĪ* (c. 870–950)
Muslim (Shīʿite?)
al-ʿĀmirī* (d. 992)
Muslim
Yaḥyā b. ʿAdī* (893/4–974)
Christian (Monophysite)
Abū Sulaymān al-Sijistānī*
(c. 913/4–c. 987/8)
Muslim
Ibn Hindū (d. c. 1019)
Muslim
Abū Ḥayyān al-Tawḥīdī*
(c. 922/32–c. 1023)
Muslim
Key
Indicates they met
Indicates a formal or informal master/disciple or student relationship
*
Authors specifically covered in this book

Figure 1 The chains of knowledge

germination and intellectual efflorescence. Shīʿism, in other words, is an integral thread in the backdrop of radical change which confronted the authors described in this book. Al-Fārābī's own Shīʿite leanings have been noted on more than one occasion.[7]

Al-Fārābī (*c.* AD 870-950)

Any description of al-Fārābī's life is problematic.[8] Unlike Ibn Sīnā,[9] he left no autobiography.[10] Furthermore, some of the primary source material is suspect.[11] The brief biography that follows is, therefore, a tentative reconstruction from a variety of primary and secondary sources:[12] it must not be regarded as definitive.

Al-Fārābī has achieved in both east and west, across the centuries, near universal acclaim for his intellectual achievements.[13] So al-ʿĀmirī strikes a unique sour note in his apparent description of al-Fārābī as 'one of the modern pseudo-philosophers' (*baʿḍ al-ḥadath min al-mutafalsifīn*).[14] Part of the problem in surveying al-Fārābī's life lies in separating the legend from the fact and making some sense of what remains despite considerable obscurities. Al-Fārābī's linguistic talents, for example, have clearly been much exaggerated. Ibn Khallikān's statement that al-Fārābī told the Ḥamdānid Prince, Sayf al-Dawla (*reg.* AD 944/5-967), that he was proficient in more than seventy languages[15] is, in Madkour's neat phrase, 'more akin to the fabulous than to exact history'.[16] Second, the true nature of al-Fārābī's much-vaunted poverty and asceticism[17] has been queried by some like Walzer. Certainly there was no guarantee that the wearing of ṣūfī or ascetic-style apparel indicated an internal ṣūfī or mystical disposition.[18] A final example of the inherent difficulties in separating the truth from the legend lies in the circumstances of al-Fārābī's death: do we, for example, accept with Ibn Abī Uṣaybiʿa, Ibn Khallikān and Ibn al-Qifṭī that he died (naturally) in Damascus?[19] Or is al-Bayhaqī's report (which maintains that al-Fārābī was attacked and killed by robbers while travelling from Damascus to Ascalon) more worthy of credence?[20] The search for the historical Fārābī, like that for the historical Jesus, goes on; and the demythologizing of al-Fārābī, at least as far as his life is concerned, is clearly a prerequisite before any *definitive* biographical sketch can be attempted. None of what has been said, however, detracts from or invalidates in any way the substance of his thought embodied in a huge multitude of writings, nor the magnitude of his intellectual achievement which those writings manifest.

The precise date of al-Fārābī's birth is unknown, but it is generally reckoned to have been around AD 870. He appears to have been born into a military family of Turkish origin in the village of Wasīj, Fārāb, in Turkestan. The details of al-Fārābī's childhood are exceedingly obscure. However, we know that he learned Arabic in Baghdad and that, later, he studied Arabic grammar with Abū Bakr ibn al-Sarrāj (*c.* AD 875–928/9). In view of al-Fārābī's expertise in logic and philosophy, perhaps the most interesting names among his teachers were those of the Nestorian Christian Yūḥannā ibn Ḥaylān (d. between AD 908 and AD 932) and the great logician Abū Bishr Mattā ibn Yūnus (d. AD 940). Ibn Khallikān claims that the majority of al-Fārābī's books were written in Baghdad;[21] but the evident attraction of this city, where he achieved fame and pre-eminence as a writer and thinker, did not prevent travel to other parts of the Arab world, most notably to Egypt, to Damascus – where he is alleged to have worked as a warden or gardener (*nāṭūr*)[22] – to Ḥarrān and to Ḥamdānid Aleppo. Although some scholars do not seem to have been unduly worried by this gardening episode,[23] Badawī has queried the reliability and plausibility of such a tale, if it took place when al-Fārābī was *already* under the patronage of Sayf al-Dawla.[24] It is quite possible that this story, like so much alleged about the life of al-Fārābī, is part of the broader myth, the attempt by later writers to establish a paradigm of an antinomian scholar-gipsy. Al-Fārābī's 'posturing' in ṣūfī garb (*bi-zayy ahl al-taṣawwuf*) at the Ḥamdānid court and elsewhere (to which we have already alluded), would fit neatly into the theory of such a paradigm.[25]

A final event in his life, which allegedly took place at the Ḥamdānid court in Aleppo, where the ruler Sayf al-Dawla had become the patron of al-Fārābī, may be adumbrated here. It is given as a last illustration of the way in which the myth keeps merging with, or at least intruding upon, the reality in any attempt at a coherent account of the philosopher's life.

That al-Fārābī became expert in both practical musicianship and theoretical musicology is beyond question.[26] Indeed, he wrote a huge work on music entitled *The Great Book of Music* (*Kitāb al-Mūsīqā al-Kabīr*);[27] but the account of his playing before the ruler at the Ḥamdānid court has clearly become embroidered with time and must surely belong to the stuff of legend. A version of what is undoubtedly the same basic story is recounted by both al-Bayhaqī and Ibn Khallikān;[28] it is the latter's account of al-Fārābī playing before Sayf al-Dawla which is translated here:

> Sayf al-Dawla dismissed them [the *ʿulamāʾ*] and remained alone with al-Fārābī. Then he said to him, 'Would you like to eat?' Al-Fārābī said, 'No.' So he said to him, 'Would you like to drink?' Al-Fārābī said, 'No.' Sayf al-Dawla said, 'Would you like to listen [to some music]?' Al-Fārābī said, 'Yes.' So Sayf al-Dawla gave orders for the singers to be brought in and each expert in this art came in with a variety of musical instruments. But each time one of them played on his instrument, al-Fārābī found fault with him, saying, 'You have made a mistake!' Then Sayf al-Dawla said to him, 'Have you any proficiency in this art?' Al-Fārābī said, 'Yes.' He then drew from his waist a leather bag (*kharīṭa*), opened it and drew from it some reeds (*ʿīdān*), which he put together. Then he played on them, whereupon all who were at the *majlis* laughed. Then he took them to pieces and put them together another way, and when he played on them, everyone in the *majlis* cried. Then he took them to pieces [yet] again, put them together differently, played on them and everyone in the *majlis*, even the doorkeeper, fell asleep. And al-Fārābī went out.[29]

One of the most fascinating aspects of this story is that a version of it is also reproduced in the *Rasāʾil* of the Ikhwān al-Ṣafāʾ,[30] which may lend some support to a theory which I have aired elsewhere about a common source for some of the writings of both al-Fārābī and the Ikhwān.[31] In the Ikhwān's account (which appears twice in the *Rasāʾil*, the first time, appropriately, at the beginning of *The Epistle on Music*), the protagonist is an unknown 'tramp' (*insān rathth 'l-ḥāl, ʿalayhi thiyāb raththa*)[32] or 'hermit-like' figure (*insān rathth 'l-ḥāl, ʿalayhi thiyāb al-nussāk*):[33]

> There are tunes and melodies which can translate souls from one state to another and change their characters from one opposite to another. An example of that is the tale which is told of a group of musical devotees who gathered at a dinner party held by a great notable. This man ranked them in his *majlis* according to their skill in their art. Then a man of shabby appearance, dressed in shabby clothes, entered, and the major-domo (lit. *ṣāḥib al-majlis*) placed him higher than all of them. Their faces exhibited their disquiet at that. The major-domo wished to demonstrate [the new guest's] superiority and calm the others' anger. So he asked him to let them hear something of his art. The man took out some pieces of wood which were with him,

> put them together and stretched [some] strings over them. He then played in such a way that it made all who were in the *majlis* laugh from the pleasure, and happiness and delight which seized their souls. Then he altered [the strings] and played a different tune which made everyone cry because of the delicacy of the melody and the sorrow which invaded their hearts. Then he altered [the strings again] and played in such a way that it sent everyone to sleep. [The man] then rose and went out and no further news was heard of him.[34]

The Ikhwān al-Ṣafā' do not give any positive name or identity to this strange, shabby Pied-Piper figure who attends the dinner in such an odd way and with such a virtuoso display of musical skill. Indeed, both this account and the one which appears later in the *Rasā'il*[35] stress that nothing further is heard of the visitor. Surely it would not be too far-fetched (depending, of course, on the date allocated to the compilation of the *Rasā'il*) to suppose that the mystery musician was al-Fārābī himself? After all, we have already noted his penchant for wearing shabby, ṣūfī-style apparel.[36] There is also a striking similarity in some of the vocabulary, as well as the narrative, between the accounts of Ibn Khallikān and the Ikhwān. Ultimately, however, this must remain a matter of conjecture.

Al-Fārābī is renowned as the author of many well-known works, notably that which is customarily abbreviated as *The Virtuous City* (*al-Madīna al-Fāḍila*). Some of these will be alluded to where necessary in the course of this book. The purpose of these few brief remarks is to present an introduction to Fārābī the man: if the account appears to lack real coherence, this is because no full chronological account is possible from the primary Arabic sources at our disposal. What we can say with some degree of certainty is that al-Fārābī's life represented a striving for order against a background of instability and change.[37] It was also the product of a highly eclectic milieu where al-Fārābī, the student of a Nestorian Christian, Yūḥannā ibn Ḥaylān, among others, inhabited the court of the Shī'ite Sayf al-Dawla. Al-Fārābī's life there represents not so much ṣūfī asceticism versus court luxury, as the (admittedly self-conscious and even posturing) independence of the free spirit, the man who has and wants little, versus the interdependence and mutual flattery of everyday court life. Philosophy represented free thinking or, better, the *freedom* to think and it was underpinned by Sayf al-Dawla's subscription to him of four dirhams a day.[38]

Yaḥyā b. ʿAdī (AD 893/4–974)

Of Yaḥyā b. ʿAdī, Ibn Abī Uṣaybiʿa wrote:

> He was supreme in his age in [intellectual] leadership and knowledge of the philosophical sciences. He studied under Abū Bishr Mattā and Abū Naṣr al-Fārābī and several others. He was unique in his time. By religion he was a Monophysite Christian (*wa madhhabuhu min madhāhib al-Naṣāra al-Yaʿqūbiyya*). He had considerable proficiency in translation and translated from Syriac into Arabic. He [also] wrote much and produced several books.[39]

Elsewhere, however, a note of caution intruded:

> The excellent Yaḥyā b. ʿAdī composed a Syriac and Arabic commentary on the Sophistic [i Elenchi]. I have seen most of it and estimate that it comprises about two-thirds of the work. I presume that he completed it, but after his death it could not be found among his books. My opinions about this fluctuate. Sometimes I think that he may have destroyed it because he was dissatisfied with it, while at other times I suspect that it was stolen, which I consider more likely. He produced the said translation before compiling his commentary, hence it is a little obscure, *for he did not always grasp the meaning correctly* and based his translation on the Syriac text.[40]

This idea that Yaḥyā's scholarship was not quite all it should have been was reiterated even more powerfully by his student Abū Ḥayyān al-Tawḥīdī who attended Yaḥyā's *majlis* and who mixed plaudits with some fairly damning and calculated indictments of his master's academic abilities:

> As for Yaḥyā b. ʿAdī, he was a mild-mannered, timid *shaykh* who was lousy at interpretation and expressed himself badly. But he was kindly in the elucidation of divergent [questions]. He outshone the majority of this group in his *majlis*. He was not a very rigorous metaphysician (lit. *wa lam yakun yalūdh bi 'l-Ilāhiyyāt*) and would become laboured[41] and make mistakes in the exposition of [metaphysics]. What was sublime [in metaphysics] was obscure to him, let alone what was subtle. [Yet] he ran a splendid salon (lit. *wa kāna mubārak al-majlis*).[42]

Modern opinion, however, has not always been as harsh as that of

Yaḥyā's contemporaries by any means. Majid Fakhry, for example, characterizes the philosopher as 'far more than a simple dragoman of Syriac-Greek learning' and believes that he

> deserves a place all his own in the narrative of philosophical and theological controversy during the tenth century. His vast erudition is shown by numerous accounts that credit him with preserving and disseminating, very often in his own handwriting, some of the more important philosophical or logical texts prized so highly by scholars and patrons of learning.[43]

In the light of these remarks then, and despite the derogatory comments of al-Tawḥīdī, we may share the surprise of Khalil Samir that the name of Yaḥyā b. ʿAdī did not find a distinguished and rightful place in the first or third volume of the new edition of the *Encyclopaedia of Islam*.[44] For even the most casual acquaintance with his works shows that, though he was a Christian, he was one whose scholarship and thought, particularly in the Aristotelian field, had an impact on the general development of tenth-century scholarship and thinkers, Christian *and* Muslim. A glance at any list of his disciples and students, of both faiths, bears immediate witness to that.[45] He might have been a Monophysite Jacobite Christian and worked from within the framework which his faith dictated, but the range of his academic education and interests, expressed in his writings, was uncircumscribed by narrowly sectarian religious boundaries.[46] We have only to note the names of two of his most distinguished teachers in Baghdad to realize the truth of this: one was the great *Muslim* al-Fārābī; the other was the *Nestorian Christian* Abū Bishr Mattā ibn Yūnus. And a brilliant man such as Yaḥyā (whatever his academic imperfections might have been), could hardly have studied under two such celebrated teachers and remained himself '*un auteur mineur*' or '*un philosophe de second ordre*'.[47]

Yaḥyā's correct full name is considered by modern scholars to have been Abū Zakariyyā Yaḥyā b. ʿAdī b. Ḥamīd b. Zakariyyā al-Takrītī,[48] though variations clearly exist.[49] He was born in Takrīt, a town roughly one hundred miles to the north of Baghdad, in AD 893 or 894 but he lived most of his life in Baghdad where he died in AD 974. By this time he had become the most distinguished Baghdadi philosopher of his age.[50] Yaḥyā was buried in the Christian Church of St Thomas in a quarter of north-west Baghdad.[51] He was succeeded as intellectual leader in that city by the equally famous Muslim thinker and philosopher Abū Sulaymān al-Sijistānī, one of his former disciples who will be considered in the course of this book and whom Endress characterizes as becoming the 'spiritus rector of the falāsifa of Baghdad after the master had died'.[52]

A less well-known fact about the life of Yaḥyā is that, like many great philosophers before and after him, it is clear that he was unable to earn his living from philosophy alone, and was obliged to support himself by copying and selling books. Anecdotes told about his job as a copyist bear witness to his prodigious labours in this field but also underline the immense intellectual substrate and apparatus which, consciously or unconsciously, must have been built up by the philosopher in his own mind, and formed a solid platform for his own writings. His was a vigorous, one-man cottage industry – by no means uncommon for a scholar – of buying, selling, collecting, copying and translating, not to mention commenting, which embraced works as diverse as those by the well-known Muslim exegete of the Qur'ān, al-Ṭabarī (AD 839–923), the great Greek philosophers Plato and Aristotle, and Yaḥyā's own master al-Fārābī, as well as much by the Muslim scholastic theologians. Indeed, it would be fair to say that Yaḥyā b. ʿAdī's work as a copyist and translator constituted the 'postgraduate' course which succeeded the 'undergraduate' studies initially undertaken in Baghdad with al-Fārābī and Abū Bishr Mattā ibn Yūnus. It was clearly vital for his own written work.[53]

This volume will assess, in due course, the contribution of Yaḥyā's own writings in a variety of fields. However, this brief biographical introduction should not end without drawing attention, again briefly, to two major and contrasting works in his corpus: first, Yaḥyā's skills as a Christian theologian are epitomized in his famous rebuttal of an anti-Trinitarian polemic by the 'Father of Islamic Philosophy', Abū Yūsuf Yaʿqūb ibn Isḥāq al-Kindī (d. after AD 866).[54] Fakhry has rightly stressed that Yaḥyā's 'standing in the history of Islamic theological thought is such that he is one of the few Christian scholars of the period to have taken an active part in theological debates with his Muslim contemporaries', and that 'he is one of the few Christian authors whose theological views are quoted or discussed by subsequent Muslim authors'.[55] Al-Kindī's original polemic is, alas, lost but it is possible to reconstruct al-Kindī's arguments with some accuracy from Yaḥyā's response.[56] The latter goes by the long title *Exposition of the Error of Abū Yūsuf Yaʿqūb ibn Isḥāq al-Kindī, in his Treatise 'A Rebuttal of the Christians' (Tabyīn Ghalaṭ Abī Yūsuf Yaʿqūb ibn Isḥāq al-Kindī fī Maqālatihā fī 'l-Radd ʿalā 'l-Naṣārā)*.[57]

Second, in one of only a small number of Arabic treatises on ethics still extant,[58] Yaḥyā b. ʿAdī shows his mastery in a quite different field: his *Refinement of Character* (*Tahdhīb al-Akhlāq*) works from the premise that man will naturally follow the evil tendencies in his nature, unless such tendencies are checked by proper 'refinement' or education of his character and morals.[59] The theme will be pursued later in this book: Yaḥyā's ethical work is simply mentioned here as a second, and contrasting, piece of scholarship to illustrate another facet of the multifarious interests of the Baghdadi philosopher.

Abū Sulaymān al-Sijistānī (*c.* AD 913/4–AD 987/8)[60]

Like Yaḥyā b. ʿAdī,[61] Abū Sulaymān al-Sijistānī also bore the title 'The Logician' (*al-Manṭiqī*).[62] Ibn Abī Uṣaybiʿa gives his full name as Abū Sulaymān Muḥammad b. Ṭāhir b. Bahrām al-Sijistānī.[63] He may be reckoned a full member of the 'School of Fārābī', or adherent of what we have termed 'Fārābism', via his acknowledged master Yaḥyā:[64] and, as we have already noted, the student succeeded the master as intellectual leader in Baghdad.

The exact dates of al-Sijistānī's birth and death remain somewhat problematic and can only be approximated. Indeed, we are rather badly informed about the whole of the philosopher's life. He appears to have spent the early part of his youth in the region which the Arabs knew as Sijistān (i.e. Sīstān) where he was born, and later studied jurisprudence. He was a member of the Ḥanafī School of Law. From the point of view of philosophical study, al-Sijistānī's most important master, apart from Yaḥyā b. ʿAdī, in Baghdad was the almost equally famed Mattā ibn Yūnus. It is unclear exactly when al-Sijistānī arrived in Baghdad but it was probably before AD 938. He joined Yaḥyā b. ʿAdī's circle and began to establish himself as one who would be ranked among the most famous philosophers in the city of Baghdad and, indeed, in his age. As a student of Yaḥyā, he eschewed textual editorial work of the kind for which Yaḥyā's circle was famed, and concentrated instead on pure philosophy.[65] Ibn al-Qifṭī alleges that al-Sijistānī was both one-eyed and suffering from leprosy, but it is clear that such reports should be treated with immense caution.[66]

Although most of his intellectual and academic life was centred on Baghdad, where he was fortunate enough to gain the support and patronage of the Būyid Prince ʿAḍud al-Dawla (*reg.* AD 978–83), he also visited the philosophical and cultural circle attached to the Ṣaffārid Abū Jaʿfar Aḥmad b. Muḥammad b. Khalaf b. al-Layth. The latter ruled as king in Sijistān from AD 923–63.[67] This kind of academic visiting bears witness not only to the frequent court patronage of scholars and intellectuals by a wide variety of rulers, but underlines also the growth of al-Sijistānī's philosophical reputation and the way in which he spread his philosophical mantle. He may indeed have visited Sijistān several times in his role of 'visiting professor' and it is fascinating to note that the group of scholars that congregated at the court there seems to have been quite distinct from the Baghdad set.[68]

Al-Sijistānī also wrote poetry but it is considered by modern scholars to be mediocre stuff. The philosopher himself seems to have been aware of his own poetic limitations.[69] It is on his philosophical *oeuvre* that his fame rests, the system of which, 'like that of most of the other members of his environment, had a strong Neo-platonic colouring'. This comment of Stern's will be developed later.[70] Unlike Ibn Sīnā and Ibn Rushd, al-Sijistānī's works did not find a Latin translator and so the scholastic Middle Ages in the west remained in ignorance of what he had written and cherished other Arab and Persian authors instead.[71] Had the Latin translators been aware of Abū Sulaymān al-Sijistānī, however, it is his *Cupboard of Wisdom* (*Ṣiwān al-Ḥikma*) which would have undoubtedly caught their attention. The considerable merits of this work have been vaunted by modern scholars,[72] containing as it does

> in principle ... innumerable dicta of 'wise men' (*ḥukamā'*), non-Muslim and Muslim, chiefly but by no means exclusively on ethical and metaphysical subjects. These are usually represented as real dicta, i.e. spoken opinions, but sometimes as quotations from a written work.... The form of the book thus presupposes a considerable period during which translations of philosophical texts were in the hands of the Arabic reading public. There is no reason to think that the dicta, even where, as is usually the case, we cannot trace them, have been invented by Abū Sulaimān. His book has plainly a derivative character, and is in fact a compilation depending on earlier sources.[73]

Further comment will, of course, be made upon this most notable of the known works of al-Sijistānī in due course.

Whether one sees Abū Sulaymān al-Sijistānī as a temporal link between al-Fārābī and Ibn Sīnā,[74] or whether one stresses that he should rather be viewed as 'a precious link in the chain of transmission of knowledge from the world of late classical antiquity to the world of Islam',[75] al-Sijistānī's place in the history of Islamic philosophy in general, and Fārābism in particular, is secure even if it is not hugely important. He may have lacked the real originality of, for example, al-Fārābī, but then so did Ibn Sīnā in several respects. He may defy neat classification and be imbued as much with the Aristotelian as the Neoplatonic.[76] And it is true that he did not have a great impact on the Islamic philosophers who came after him.[77] His significance, as Kraemer stresses, lies in his being part of a chain of knowledge and an epitome of the learning of his age. It is for this last aspect that he is of value to us for study in this volume and it is, therefore, from this perspective that we will later survey his work, unhampered by considerations of greatness or otherwise in the hierarchy of Islamic philosophers.[78]

A final theme, or question, in al-Sijistānī's life might be considered here which is also a theme informing some of what follows in this volume: what is the relationship between philosophy and knowledge, on the one hand, and life, particularly in its political aspects, on the other? The theme, or question, is clearly underpinned by the fact of patronage, financial or otherwise, which so many worldly political figures gave to poets and scholars, almost as a kind of intellectual variant on the almsgiving, voluntary and obligatory, enjoined by Islam. Salvation, according to this paradigm, was achieved for the ruler or politician by his support of an academic elite rather than a downtrodden underworld which lacked the brain or influence to tease from that ruler a few dinars, or at least his respect and protection.[79]

Al-Sijistānī's response was uncompromising, at least after the *death* of a benefactor! Philosophy was the only true 'way of life' and courtly patronage could not be allowed to obscure the correct philosophical attitude towards political power. As Abū Sulaymān said when ʿAḍud al-Dawla died, and his philosophical coterie re-enacted the scene of the ten philosophers round the coffin of Alexander the Great: 'This person weighed this world improperly, assigning it an excessive value. Suffice it to say that seeking gain in this world he lost his soul.'[80]

Abū 'l-Ḥasan Muḥammad b. Yūsuf al-ʿĀmirī (d. AD 992)

Whatever al-ʿĀmirī's view of al-Fārābī,[81] there can be no doubt about the impact which the latter had on the former as far as al-ʿĀmirī's writings were concerned.[82] Like al-Sijistānī, therefore, he ranks as a member of what we are terming the 'School of Fārābī' and it is from this point of view that he will primarily be considered in this volume. Indeed, he has much in common with al-Sijistānī: like him 'he employs a fine Arabic style with an abundance of Persian maxims or Greek apophthegms; like him, he is in search of a Neoplatonic formula which will suit his age and his nation'.[83] A final, more obvious, point of similarity which might be mentioned here is that both philosophers inhabited the age of the Būyids which has been described neatly as 'eminently a period of tensions and controversies of which the echo, however feeble, reaches us through the works of Miskawayh and al-Tawḥīdī'. Vadet asks whether it is necessary to state that it is religion 'principally conceived in a Persian fashion under its philosophical aspect' which is at the heart of both debate and joust.[84]

Al-ʿĀmirī was born in an early part of the tenth century AD in Nīsābūr (Nishapur). Not a great deal is known about his early life, though we do know that he studied under the famous Abū Zayd al-Balkhī (*c.* AD 850–934) who was skilled in both geography and philosophy. Of this al-Balkhī, Vadet has written: 'Our Khurasanian philosopher was as a matter of fact a disciple of the famous Abū Zayd Aḥmad b. Sahl al-Balkhī, an essayist who wrote on a variety of subjects, a man of diverse propensities, a complex personality'.[85]

Later, in Rayy, al-ʿĀmirī gained the patronage of the Būyid *wazīr* Abū 'l-Fadl b. al-ʿAmīd (d. AD 970) and that of Ibn al-ʿAmīd's son who succeeded his father and was called Abū 'l-Fatḥ Dhū 'l-Kifāyatayn (d. AD 976). After visits to Baghdad in AD 970/1 and 974/5, al-ʿĀmirī was back in Khurāsān by AD 980. He is known to have been writing in Bukhārā in AD 985/6 and to have died in Nīsābūr in AD 992.

Perhaps the most interesting period of his life is that which he spent in Baghdad and about which we are better informed. It is clear that he made himself extremely unpopular with the resident Baghdad philosophers. It remains a matter of debate whether this was due to a genuine 'provincial' behaviour on the part of al-ʿĀmirī, or to a closed-circle elitist and coterie mentality, which might at that time have been hostile to 'outsiders' like al-ʿĀmirī. Al-Tawḥīdī's view of the philosopher was somewhat ambivalent: he was characterized as one who, because of his tediousness, boorish nature and harsh character (*li-kazāzatihi wa ghilaẓ ṭibāʿihi wa jafā' khuluqihi*), frightened others away.[86] Clearly, however, a large amount of xenophobia lurked beneath the sophisticated philosophical veneer of Baghdad. It is equally clear that the contempt felt by the Baghdadis for al-ʿĀmirī was reciprocated in abundance.[87]

Al-ʿĀmirī was a prolific author with more than seventeen works to his credit.[88] Of these, three are of particular interest and will be referred to in greater or lesser detail in the course of this book: (i) *On Being Happy and Causing Happiness* (*Kitāb al-Saʿāda wa 'l-Isʿād*);[89] (ii) *On Making Known the Virtues of Islam* (*Kitāb al-Iʿlām bi Manāqib al-Islām*); and (iii) *On the Afterlife* (*Kitāb al-Amad ʿalā 'l-Abad*). (The translation of the Arabic title here is Rowson's: see the Bibliography.) The study and publication of such works has served to revive al-ʿĀmirī's once flagging reputation.[90] *On Being Happy* is important, however, because, as well as constituting a welcome addition to known treatises on Islamic political philosophy, it is, in Arberry's words, full of valuable 'quotations from Greek and Sassanian sources, some of which are otherwise lost. [This] gives the work of Abū l-Ḥasan ibn Abī Dharr [al-ʿĀmirī][91] considerable value.' Arberry concluded his remarks by saying that he knew 'of no other Arabic writer who cites Aristotle and Plato so freely and so accurately'.[92]

Yet al-ʿĀmirī is not just a Platonist or Aristotelian; his philosophy is an 'amalgam of Neoplatonism and Aristotelianism' even if done in 'a rather conventional' way.[93] Such combinations were not uncommon: The *Epistles* (*Rasā'il*) of the Brethren of Purity (*Ikhwān al-Ṣafā'*) provide an excellent example of a text infused with both Aristotelianism and Neoplatonism. And if *On Being Happy* represents the Aristotelian aspect of this, then *On the Afterlife* emphatically and directly represents the Neoplatonic,[94] written as it was 'to validate the notion of immortality, or rather resurrection (*al-qiyāma*)'.[95]

Finally, *On Making Known the Virtues of Islam*, al-ʿĀmirī's philosophical defence of Islam, is a notable work of apologetic which is

> as much the witness of a conscience as an ideological and historical achievement. This witness implies a constant toil throughout an austere and rather rugged life, and perhaps also the existence of a philosophical tradition nearer to Islam than that of the philosophers (*falāsifa*).[96]

The three volumes briefly described above illustrate three different facets of al-ʿĀmirī's thought: the Platonic and Aristotelian, the Neoplatonic and the philosophically apologetic. However, there is a fourth and final one which deserves to be touched upon here since it sets al-ʿĀmirī apart from some, but not all, his brother philosophers. This is the ṣūfī dimension of his life and thought.

Mysticism and philosophy have frequently taken root in the same mind throughout the long history of intellectual development in the Near and Middle East. One has only to think of the great Ibn Sīnā

(AD 979–1037) and, after him, al-Suhrawardī (AD 1153–91) and Ibn al-ʿArabī (AD 1165–1240), to realize the truth of this. Al-ʿĀmirī appears from the evidence not to have belonged to a particular ṣūfī order (*ṭarīqa*), but to have been an itinerant ṣūfī.[97] Kraemer holds that al-ʿĀmirī was part of an intellectual tradition which merged a native ṣūfī asceticism with a Platonic philosophical elitism.[98] This tradition must have been elaborated in a book which he is known to have written on ṣūfism.[99]

In the light of all this, it is perhaps clearer why al-ʿĀmirī disturbed the cosy status quo of the Baghdad philosophers. But perhaps, also, as Rowson suggests, the principal reason why al-ʿĀmirī and his fellow philosophers fell out was that while the latter wished to preserve a division between philosophy and Islam, al-ʿĀmirī wanted to bring the two closer together and persuade the *ʿulamāʾ* to approve of philosophy with a positive spirit.[100]

Abū Ḥayyān al-Tawḥīdī (*c.* AD 922–32 to *c.* AD 1023)

ʿAlī b. Muḥammad b. al-ʿAbbās Abū Ḥayyan al-Tawḥīdī was one of the most dynamic and informative members of the group which we have termed the 'School of Fārābī'. His name derives not from the Arabic word indicating a belief in the absolute unity of God (*tawḥīd*) but from its homonym which denotes a species of Iraqi dates.[101]

Abū Ḥayyān's place of birth is uncertain. It may have been in places as far apart as Baghdad, Shīrāz, Nīsābūr or Wāsiṭ. We are similarly ill-informed of his early life and adolescence. What is known is that he later studied grammar and Shāfiʿī law in Baghdad, as well as philosophy. His most important masters in the latter field were Yaḥyā b. ʿAdī, whose lectures he attended in AD 971, and Abū Sulaymān al-Sijistānī.

Exactly when Abū Ḥayyān arrived for the first time in Baghdad is also uncertain. However, he seems to have regarded this as his principal base throughout his life, though he made several forays to other places: we find him in Mecca, for example, in AD 963, and later, in Rayy where, in AD 977, he commenced a three-year tour of duty in the employment of the Muʿtazilī *wazīr* al-Ṣāḥib Ibn ʿAbbād (AD 938–95). George Hourani characterizes the latter as 'himself a talented scholar and writer but more notable as a wealthy and generous patron of letters'.[102] The *wazīr* and the secretary-courtier al-Tawḥīdī did not get on together and their mutual animosity is described in a number of anecdotes. As Kraemer puts it:

Again he met with disappointment. As usual, his talents were unappreciated. He was forced to do the menial and dreary work of a copyist, an employment which, as he put it, was hardly lacking in Baghdad. He clashed with his patron on personal and doctrinal grounds. He vented his spleen against the viziers, Ibn al-ʿAmīd and Ibn ʿAbbād, in his *Akhlāq* (or *Dhamm* or *Mathālib*) *al-Wazīrayn* [*The Character* or *Censure* or *Defects of the Two Wazīrs*], wherein the faults of the two viziers are recounted.[103]

Al-Tawḥīdī made an impecunious return to Baghdad in AD 980 where he first found employment in a hospital and then with the *wazīr* Ibn Saʿdān (d. AD 984), the *wazīr* who figures in Abū Ḥayyān's most famous work, *The Book of Pleasure and Conviviality* (*Kitāb al-Imtāʿ wa 'l-Mu'ānasa*), which has been accurately viewed as 'a kind of philosophical *Arabian Nights*'.[104] Now his fortunes took a turn for the better: 'From lowly copyist he rose to the proud station of constant boon-companion at the soirées of Ibn Saʿdān.'[105]

However, Ibn Saʿdān's execution in AD 984 meant that Abū Ḥayyān was left with no strong protector or patron. The last years of his life resemble his first in that we know very little about them. He left Baghdad and went into retirement in Shīrāz, burning his books in a fever of ascetic piety. He appears to have fallen on hard times and to have died a somewhat embittered and disappointed man in AD 1023.[106]

It is possible that Abū Ḥayyān may have been responsible, to a certain extent, for the woes that beset him. As we have already noted, he was clearly not an easy man to get on with. He fell out with at least two *wazīr*s and his fault-finding and extreme pessimism make him appear an unlovely character. Furthermore, his tactlessness, unsuitable dress at court and general inexperience cannot have endeared him to the great. Yet they, at least, clearly endured him. He was of use with his wide-ranging knowledge of things intellectual and political and he also had a tremendous entertainment value.[107] Such factors must explain, at least in part, his relationship with the *wazīr* Ibn Saʿdān. The literary result of the *wazīr*'s patience and curiosity on the one hand, and Abū Ḥayyān's abusive nature and love of gossip on the other, was *The Book of Pleasure and Conviviality*.

Writing about this work, Stern stressed its importance as a veritable mine of information about the thriving intellectual milieu inhabited by Abū Ḥayyān; he also believed that this work would 'prove invaluable for a reconstruction of the doctrines of the Baghdad philosophers'.[108] These remarks have been underlined by other scholars like Mahjoub, who also believes that *The Book of Pleasure and Conviviality* provides an excellent reflection of the personality of Abū Ḥayyān himself.[109]

We have already referred to the author's scurrilousness and general inability to live tactfully and graciously in the courts of some of his patrons. A final facet of his personality should, however, be mentioned here which is somewhat unexpected in the light of the above. Like al-ʿĀmirī, Abū Ḥayyān was interested in mysticism. Such an interest may, of course, explain both his lack of dress sense and his final retreat to the ṣūfī stronghold of Shīrāz in his old age.[110]

Al-Tawḥīdī is known to have studied with ṣūfī masters. On his pilgrimage to Mecca in AD 963, ṣūfīs were his chosen companions.[111] Stern, after noting Abū Ḥayyān's Neoplatonic interests, adds that his interest in ṣūfism, however, was 'not enough to make him a regular ṣūfī'.[112] Kraemer places a more profound stress on Abū Ḥayyān's ṣūfism and accepts that, because of his attraction to Neoplatonism, the term 'philosophico-mystic', coined by Anawati and Gardet, is a suitable one to apply to him.[113] Certainly, his life and thought were an eclectic mixture which truly encapsulated 'the era's insecurity and its vanity, its self-doubt and its arrogance'.[114] It was stressed earlier that the Age of Fārābism was an age of deep instability and change. Some scholars clearly embraced ṣūfism as a reaction to, or haven from, such factors. Others, like al-Tawḥīdī, began as, and remained, ṣūfīs throughout their lives while engaging at the same time in the practice of sundry other avocations like those of philosopher, courtier, writer, secretary, gossip and scandalmonger! The incomparable value of Abū Ḥayyān al-Tawḥīdī for this volume lies, however, not in the fact that he gloried in embracing and combining all these different 'careers' in the one single person of himself; but, rather, that such an amalgam of differing careers gave him an entrée to the salons and *majālis* – literary, political and cultural – of those who had real power and thus provided him with the primary material for one of the most important documents of the age, *The Book of Pleasure and Conviviality*.

Court Culture, Conviviality and *Kalām*

It is clear from the briefest acquaintance with the Age of Fārābism, and, indeed, much of the Islamic Middle Ages, that there was a considerable interaction between the general court culture and the learning of the day. By 'court culture' I mean not simply the milieu of those right at the top of the hierarchy of medieval Islamic society like the caliph, king or prince but also that of the slightly lower echelons such as their ministers. Certain princes and *wazīrs* stand out as sublime patrons of the arts, and under their aegis philosophy, theology, poetry and *belles-lettres* flourished. And while there might be an official 'party line' from a religious point of view, embraced by the ruler and commanding the nominal adherence of those below him to a greater or lesser degree, this did not always inhibit the views of the intellectuals who inhabited the court milieu. The religious tolerance (or, better, indifference?) of the Būyids, for example, has already been noted. Of course, this tolerance was not always the case with every ruler. An age slightly previous to the one which is the focus of this book had undergone the trauma of the *miḥna* or inquisition in which the ʿAbbāsid Caliph al-Ma'mūn (*reg.* AD 813–33) had endeavoured to impose the heterodox doctrines of Muʿtazilite theology by brute force. Independently minded jurists, scholars and theologians, like the great Aḥmad b. Ḥanbal (AD 780–855), had suffered grievously as a result.

What follows in this section will attempt briefly to survey, and give a flavour of, general court culture ranging in the process over the entire Islamic Middle Ages and not just the Age of Fārābism. It will note how that culture embraced, or interacted with, the wit and popular wisdom of the times as well as higher learning, *kalām* and philosophy (epitomized in such thinkers as the five who are the principal subjects of this work).

First, however, it is useful to try and disentangle four not always discrete paradigms or models of the interaction of court culture and intellectual or popular narrative activity, relevant both to the age prior to the Age of Fārābism and to that of Fārābism itself (which runs, as we have suggested, from AD 870 until AD 1023).

The first, deriving from the popular and, admittedly, justified view of the early ʿAbbāsid era as a golden age of intellectual expansion and achievement, may be termed *the exotic paradigm.* According to this rather naïve model, the ages are filtered through the sieve of popular literary works like *The Thousand and One Nights.* The court may seem at times to exist only to be the frame or milieu of entertaining wit, narration, enquiry or debate, presided over by the sometimes ambivalent genius of this or that intellectual ruler. Now the reality may *occasionally* have matched the myth, but the actual history of the ʿAbbāsid era, for example, hardly persuades us that the exotic paradigm was the norm. In *The Thousand and One Nights,* we find the ʿAbbāsid Caliph

Hārūn al-Rashīd (*reg.* AD 786–809), for instance, clearly suffering from insomnia, commanding his *wazīr* thus:

> 'O Jafar, tonight my breast is heavy for lack of sleep. I charge you with the lightening of it'. 'Commander of the Faithful', answered Jafar, 'I have a friend called Alī the Persian, who has in his scrip many delicious tales which are sovereign remedies for the blackest humours and annoyances'. 'Bring him to me at once', said al-Rashīd, and when Jafar had obeyed and the man was seated in the presence, he continued: 'Listen, Alī, I am told that you know stories which can dissipate weariness and bring sleep to the sleepless. I require one of them now'. 'I hear and obey, O Prince of Believers', answered Alī the Persian. 'I pray you tell me whether you wish a story of things heard or a tale of things seen with my own eyes?'. 'One in which you have taken part yourself', said Hārūn al-Rashīd.[115]

This is a typical frame story from what has been termed 'the Hārūn Cycle' in *The Thousand and One Nights*. Of this cycle, Mia Gerhardt has observed:

> It glorifies the caliph and his reign; it calls up, now in bold outline and now in minute detail, a splendid picture that is artistically as convincing as it is historically untrue.... On the whole, history does not count him among the great caliphs. But his time was economically prosperous and culturally brilliant.[116]

How much of the cultural brilliance and wit as portrayed in such works as *The Thousand and One Nights* and ineluctably associated with Hārūn and his court was actually true, and how much belonged only to the narrator's art, can only be guessed at. What we *can* say is that it is as a result of such literature, regarded in however lowly a fashion, that what I have termed 'the exotic paradigm' came into being, where the picture of court culture purveyed was one of a constant interaction of wit, humour, entertainment as well as intellect, at the expense of much else.

Of course, the story-teller did have his role, a respected role which he fulfilled in front of a lone individual, a small group or a large gathering; *majālis* or literary salons *were* held. The *wazīr* Ibn Saʿdān did, in some senses at least, play the role of King Shahryār to al-Tawḥīdī's Shahrazād. And, as we have already seen, al-Tawḥīdī's famous *Book of Pleasure and Conviviality* has been described as 'a kind of philosophical *Arabian Nights*'.[117] But the reality was not all a bed of roses. It was, rather, what I will term as a second paradigm, *the paradigm of patronage.* That reality could be an uneasy symbiosis between artist and court patron, with an eventual destruction of the relationship and consequent possible threat to the life itself of that client-artist. For example, al-Tawḥīdī maintained good relations with Ibn Saʿdān and esteemed that *wazīr*, but he had previously fallen out with other important patrons.

Third, there was what followed on from the paradigm of patronage, and was frequently connected to it: it might usefully be called here *the sycophants' paradigm.* In effect, a crude reality often lurked behind the patron's good will: a praise-poem for a bag of gold! Major poets, as well as minor, were not immune from both sycophancy and self-interest. The following examples will illustrate this in full measure. While Abū 'l-ʿAlā' al-Maʿarrī (AD 973–1057), the great blind poet of medieval Syria, might claim to be immune from the temptation of writing verse for reward,[118] others, equally famous, were not so scrupulous. His poetic peer, the renowned al-Mutanabbī (AD 915–65), who worked under the patronage of the Ḥamdānid Prince Sayf al-Dawla, had no qualms about lauding his patron on a variety of occasions. For example, praising the prince on his departure from Antioch, al-Mutanabbī wrote:

Whither do you intend, great prince?
We are the herbs of the hills, and you are the clouds;

. . . .

Every life you do not grace is death;
every sun that you are not is darkness.[119]

When he heard that Sayf al-Dawla had recovered from an illness, he was equally complimentary:

Glory and nobility were preserved when you were preserved
and the pain passed from you to your enemies;

. . . .

I do not single out you alone for felicitation on recovery;
when you are safe and sound, all men are safe and sound.[120]

Al-Mutanabbī's poetry seems sometimes almost consciously designed to squeeze money out of his princely patron: on one occasion he recited a poem with a verse containing fourteen successive imperatives:

Pardon, bestow, endow, mount, raise, console, restore,
Add, laugh, rejoice, bring nigh, show favour, gladden, give.[121]

We are told that Sayf al-Dawla was so pleased by this that he proceeded to grant each request. For example, to answer the imperative 'bestow', the prince gave orders that al-Mutanabbī should be given a certain amount of money.[122] On other occasions, the demand was even less subtle, more direct and filled with an abundance of self-interest, as where al-Mutanabbī instructed his patron:

Reward me, whenever a poem is recited to you,
for it is only with my poetry repeated that the panegyrists
come to you;
and disregard every voice but mine,
for I am the caller who is imitated, and the other is the echo.[123]

Al-Mutanabbī was patronized and esteemed by Sayf al-Dawla for nine happy years, from AD 948 to 957, until finally (and inevitably?) he fell out with the prince and fled to Egypt.[124] Perhaps the mutual symbiosis was ultimately self-destructive.

I have spent some time delineating the relationships and interaction between the Ḥamdānid court and literary culture, and between the prince as patron and poet as panegyrist, because they provide an excellent illustration of the third paradigm, which was identified above and given the name the sycophants' paradigm. It is worth remembering also that it was within the shadow of this milieu that the first of our authors, al-Fārābī, lived and worked, though the philosopher seems to conform rather less to the sycophants' paradigm than does the poet whom we have just surveyed. None the less, it is clear from the tale of the musicians outlined earlier in this chapter that al-Fārābī could be relied upon to provide some form of unexpected entertainment at the court of Sayf al-Dawla, from whom he received, we are told, a stipend of four silver dirhams a day.[125] Despite the much-vaunted ṣūfī clothing, it is clear that al-Fārābī was in receipt of rather more than just 'subsistence patronage'. Walzer comments: 'He was content to live on a salary of four silver dirhams a day – this is, as I learn … "well above subsistence level for a peasant (who could probably manage on two dirhams per month)" but not enough to cut a respectable figure as a member of the middle or upper classes.' Walzer concludes: 'Al-Fārābī evidently did not give up his principles when he decided to join this illustrious court society.'[126] Be that as it may, and whatever the relative emphasis one places on his lifestyle and dress, it is clear that al-Fārābī was as much a part of the patronage network as al-Mutanabbī, even if he was less prepared to 'sell himself' than was the poet. The two, in their very different ways, exhibit neatly the variety in the interaction between court and artist.

The paradigm of patronage and the related sycophants' paradigm by no means declined with the death of such men as Sayf al-Dawla; nor were they confined to such areas as Aleppo or, indeed, the Middle East. If we move forward a few centuries, we find that intrepid traveller and globe-trotter Ibn Baṭṭūṭa (AD 1304–1368/9 or 1377) joyfully and naturally recording aspects of both paradigms in the account of his sojourn in India at the court of the despotic and bloodthirsty ruler of Delhi, Muḥammad ibn Tughluq (*reg.* AD 1325–51). And just as al-Mutanabbī wrote praise-poems for Sayf al-Dawla in return for reward and money (the sycophants' paradigm), and later fell out with his patron and fled (the paradigm of patronage), so too did Ibn Baṭṭūṭa at the court of Delhi first praise and then withdraw from Muḥammad ibn Tughluq's service, having been first alarmingly detained and then released by that ruler.[127] The following is an example of what he wrote for the Sultan of Delhi, confidently expecting that the latter would help him with debts which Ibn Baṭṭūṭa had incurred:

> Commander of the Faithful, lord revered,
> To thee we come, through deserts toward thee hasting.
> A pilgrim I, thy glory's shrine to visit,
> A refuge meet for sanctuary thy dwelling.
> Had majesty a rank above the sun,
> Fit pattern wert thou for its most excelling.
> Thou art the Imam, unique and glorious, ever
> Thy words infallibly with deeds investing.
> I am in need, thy bounty's overflow
> My hope, and by thy greatness eased my questing.
> Shall I declare it – or thy blush suffice?
> – To say 'thy bounty's plash' were seemlier punning.
> Make speed to aid the votary to thy shrine,
> And pay his debt – the creditors are dunning.[128]

Muḥammad ibn Tughluq liked the poem and agreed to help Ibn Baṭṭūṭa with his debt; but, as ill-luck would have it, circumstances conspired to delay the award of the money until much later.[129]

Poets, scholars and, indeed, travellers like Ibn Baṭṭūṭa were thus immensely conscious, in every generation of the early and later

Islamic Middle Ages, of the debt which they owed to a princely patron. Thus the death of a generous patron was a cause for real grief. When the Barmakid family was suddenly overthrown in AD 803 by the Caliph Hārūn al-Rashīd,[130] the poetry clique bitterly lamented the family's downfall, with good reason:

> The activity of the Barmakids was not merely political and administrative. An important cultural and artistic achievement is also due to them. Indeed, they acted as patrons of poets, *distributing rewards for their panegyrics* through the intermediary of a special office created specifically for the purpose, the *dīwān al-shiʿr*; they favoured scholars and gathered theologians and philosophers in their home, in assemblies (*madjālis*) which have remained famous.[131]

The following are examples of the typical, but almost ludicrously inflated, eulogies which followed from the poets' lips after the overthrow of the Barmakids. Even a superficial examination reveals that self-interest is never far from the surface:

(1) Al-Raqāshī[132] says concerning the Barmakīs...
Say too to munificence, 'After Faḍl,[133] cease completely!'
and say to calamities, 'Manifest yourselves anew every day!'

. . . .

If perfidious Time betrays us, well, it has
betrayed Jaʿfar[134] and Muḥammad,[135]
To the point that, when daylight gleamed bright, it revealed
the killing of the noblest one who has ever perished and who
had not yet been laid in his grave.

. . . .

O house of Barmak, how many a gift and act of munificence
of yours
have there been, as abundant as grains of sand, given
ungrudgingly![136]

(2) Sayf b. Ibrāhīm[137] says concerning them,
The stars of munificent gifts have set, the hand of bountifulness
has dried up,
and the seas of liberality have become scanty after the Barmakīs.
Stars of the sons of Barmak have set,
by which the camel driver used to know the direction of the way
(i.e., to the Barmakīs' liberality).[138]

Having raised the subject of the Barmakids, perhaps this is a useful point at which to adumbrate our fourth and final paradigm, to be termed *the ideal paradigm*, as a final illustration of the different and subtle kinds of interaction between court and culture in medieval Islam. The example here is taken from the description of a literary salon held by the Barmakid *wazīr* to Hārūn al-Rashīd, Yaḥyā b. Khālid al-Barmakī (d. AD 805), which was lovingly reconstructed, recorded – and probably idealized – by the great Arab historian al-Masʿūdī (*c.* AD 896–*c.* 956). While it is obvious from the selection of indifferent panegyrics quoted above that the Barmakids indeed had a mercenary relationship with the men of culture such as the poets, and turned the latter's praise poetry into bags of gold and other rewards, the same accusation cannot be levelled at the session described by al-Masʿūdī, even though a Barmakid is involved as prime instigator. Here the inherent tension in the relationship is not primarily praise poetry written for money but a mutual intellectual respect between the *wazīr* and the academy of scholars, coupled with a non-inquisitorial and liberal atmosphere where it is clear that all views – orthodox and heterodox – will at least receive a hearing. While this *majlis*, of course, takes place several generations before the Age of Fārābism (which is the primary temporal focus of this book, running as it does from AD 870 to 1023), yet it must have been duplicated frequently in many another court and meeting-place during that Fārābian Age. For example, the *majālis* held by that later *wazīr* to the Būyids, Ibn Saʿdān, in which al-Tawḥīdī was involved and whose details he recorded in *The Book of Pleasure and Conviviality*, were the obvious successors to those presided over by Yaḥyā b. Khālid al-Barmakī in an earlier period.

Al-Masʿūdī's account opens with a description of Yaḥyā himself: he is a man of scientific and intuitive knowledge, a perspicacious scholar, in whose previous literary salons many of the great theological, philosophical and political questions of the age have been aired. The discussions have been underpinned by the technical terminology of Aristotle as well as the more Islamic science of *ḥadīth*. Now the *wazīr* declares that he wishes to move to a fresh subject, that of passionate love (*ʿishq*) and he invites each of the assembled scholars to say a few words on the subject. The diversity of religious traditions to which these scholars adhere is extraordinary: Yaḥyā is answered, among others, by two Shīʿites, a Khārijite, and two Muʿtazilites and there are some glittering names indeed among the speakers. The whole *majlis* prompts al-Masʿūdī himself then to investigate the subject of passionate love, which he does with some panache, citing the Qur'ān, ḥadīth, Hippocrates, Galen, the Baghdad ṣūfīs and the famous Arab poet Jamīl b. ʿAbd Allāh b. Maʿmar al-ʿUdhrī (*c.* AD 660–701) in the process, as well as delineating ideas derived from Plato's *Symposium*, though without any formal acknowledgement of his source.[139] The whole passage, precipitated by the account of Yaḥyā's brilliant *majlis*, is a *tour de force* of medieval Islamic learning, mingling as it does the themes of love, death, and humoral medicine.[140] And indeed, if antecedents be sought both for the discussions at Yaḥyā's *majlis* and for the consequent musings of al-Masʿūdī, one could do worse than examine the *Symposium* of Plato, to which we have just referred, which also has much to say on the themes of love, death and medicine. Indeed, the sorts of Socratic gatherings which gave rise to so many of Plato's philosophical dialogues could rightly be labelled as the true Greek prototypes of the *majālis* in which Yaḥyā and Ibn Saʿdān – two widely differing types of latter-day Socrates – later engaged.

There is a curious irony in the parallelism and suddenness of the fates which both Yaḥyā and Ibn Saʿdān – men who mixed in their own lives both politics and culture – met at the hands of the rulers they served. Yaḥyā died in AD November 805, a prisoner of Hārūn al-Rashīd. Ibn Saʿdān was executed in AD 984 by the Būyid Ṣamṣām al-Dawla (*reg.* AD 983–7).[141] One aspect of the paradigm of patronage, if that phrase might be applied this time to the relationship between prince and *wazīr*, had reared its head in a particularly acute form! It is clear that, of the two *wazīr*s Yaḥyā b. Khālid al-Barmakī and Ibn Saʿdān, the former was the more able from the political point of view, though they probably had an equivalent appreciation and love of high culture. Ibn Saʿdān served as a *wazīr* to the Būyid Ṣamṣām al-Dawla from AD 983 to 984. By contrast, 'Yaḥyā remained in office for seventeen years, from 170/786 to 187/803, this period being referred to by some authors as "the reign of the Barmakids" (*sulṭān Āl Barmak*). Engaged in "righting wrongs" in the name of the caliph, he was likewise empowered to choose his own secretaries, who acted as his delegates, and was in practice head of the administration; even the office of the Seal, initially withheld from him, was soon placed under his control. Tradition likewise has it that al-Rashīd handed his personal seal over to him, a symbol of the new authority enjoyed by the *wazīr*.'[142] Ibn Saʿdān was clearly not in this league: Kraemer does not rank him among the great *wazīr*s of the period, though he pays tribute to his learning and love of scholarly company, whatever the exaggerations of al-Tawḥīdī.[143] But Kraemer concludes that 'the virtues that made Ibn Saʿdān a worthy Muslim, and the talents that made him a suitable partner in learned discourse, did not help him govern, or cope with intrigue. The economic crisis that beset his administration, and the conspiracies that entangled him, subdued this decent man.'[144] Just as Yaḥyā b. Khālid al-Barmakī and the rest of the Barmakid family must ultimately have been perceived as an economic and political threat to the ʿAbbāsid Caliph Hārūn al-Rashīd himself, so too, in a later age, was Ibn Saʿdān similarly perceived by the Būyid Prince Ṣamṣām al-Dawla.[145] Those two courtly *wazīr*s, custodians of intellectual fashion and taste, patrons of poets and scholars, whose lives were often literally at their mercy, were themselves finally, and almost ineluctably, the victims of a higher patronage!

Such then was the sometimes dangerous court milieu in which the courtiers, poets and scholars of the age lived, worked and often died. The above paragraphs provide some indication, in the midst of this, of the actual interaction between court and culture. This chapter will conclude by surveying and examining briefly the official, and quasi-official, attitudes of some of those courts with regard to religion and the preservation, or propagation, of 'orthodox' and other theologies.

I propose to examine here, in turn, as short case studies, the courts of four of the major dynasties with which the five major thinkers surveyed in this volume frequently interacted: those of the Ḥamdānids, the Būyids, the Ṣaffārids and the Sāmānids. Within the portals of their courts flourished one – or sometimes more – of five major Islamic traditions: Zaydī Shīʿism, Imāmī Shīʿism, Ismāʿīlī Shīʿism, Muʿtazilism and Sunnism. And adherents of one persuasion were not necessarily intolerant of those belonging to another; far from it! Furthermore, as must already be clear from this chapter, some of these dynasties ruled in more than one region, and thereby possessed an increased capacity for political, religious and intellectual influence, as well as tolerance or intolerance.

When one surveys the configuration of Middle Eastern states and their dynasties in the Age of Fārābism, which we have identified as being between AD 870 and 1023, it is quite astonishing to note the dominance, or, at the very least, the permeation of Shīʿite thought in one mode or another. Having itemized various Shīʿite dynasties like the Fāṭimids in Egypt, the Ḥamdānids in Syria and the Qarāmiṭa in

Bahrain, Kraemer comments: 'Shīʿī ascendancy on such a significant scale was unprecedented and unrepeated in Islamic history.'[146] He concludes that the different Shīʿī regimes

> never made an effort to unite or even to impose their confessional preference upon the Sunnī population. But they were responsible in large measure for the intensive cultural expansion that went on. And the remarkable openness and readiness for the alien and the novel may perhaps be ascribed to their confessional orientation. This intellectual Shīʿism, then, which held the political reins while Shīʿī theology and jurisprudence were being formulated, was largely responsible for the intensive cultural activity which the Renaissance of Islam witnessed.[147]

The Ḥamdānid court at Aleppo was Imāmī Shīʿite.[148] The Ḥamdānid Prince Sayf al-Dawla inherited his father's Shīʿite tendencies and surrounded himself with a circle of luminaries, including the great al-Fārābī and al-Mutanabbī, who often shared his Shīʿite religious tastes.[149] Despite his Shīʿism, however, Sayf al-Dawla was able to pose 'as a champion of Islam against the military might of the Byzantine empire'.[150] Kennedy does not find this in any way odd: 'Compared with the inaction or indifference of other Muslim rulers, it is not surprising that Sayf al-Dawla's popular reputation remained high; he was the one man who attempted to defend the Faith, the essential hero of the time.'[151] Viewed like this, Sayf al-Dawla begins to resemble a prototype Ṣalāḥ al-Dīn (Saladin), though appearing in Shīʿī garb rather than the Sunnism of the latter. That was not, however, important by comparison with his enthusiasm for the transcending factor of *jihād*.[152]

The Būyids of the Baghdad inhabited by Yaḥyā b. ʿAdī, al-Sijistānī, and al-Tawḥīdī were generally endowed with a religious tolerance, probably deriving more from the relatively recent conversion of the Būyids to Islam and their comparative theological illiteracy than from any clearly formulated and articulated policy of religious freedom and toleration.[153] It is well known that the Būyids were Shīʿites, but of which variety? It seems that originally the dynasty was Zaydī[154] but may later, at various times, have inclined towards the Imāmī branch of Shīʿism, even if such an orientation was not made official.[155] Politically, the Būyids have been described as Imāmīs.[156] Kraemer insists that an important aspect of all this was that Imāmī Shīʿism had a catalytic effect on other types of Shīʿism, notably the Ismāʿīlī variety.[157] And the general tolerance exhibited by the Būyids went beyond the boundaries of just the various types of Shīʿism. ʿAḍud al-Dawla, who ruled as Būyid prince in Baghdad from AD 978 to 983 and was the patron of Abū Sulaymān al-Sijistānī, displayed a particular tolerance for non-Muslims, employing several Christians in his entourage.[158] Such tolerance may have borne fruit in ostensibly unlikely quarters: for example, al-Tawḥīdī, though officially opposed to Shīʿism, may have been rather less hostile than is sometimes imagined. Indeed, it is just possible that he had some real contacts with Ismāʿīlism.[159]

It is interesting that, when we turn to the Būyid court at Rayy, visited by both al-Tawḥīdī and al-ʿĀmirī, there is discernible among some of the courtiers a predilection for things Muʿtazilite. The *wazīr*, Ibn ʿAbbād, whom al-Tawḥīdī came to dislike so intensely, worked here, combining adherence to Zaydism and Muʿtazilī theology.[160] The Muʿtazila of Baṣra and Baghdad were able to gain a third major centre in Rayy as a result of the appointment of such scholars as the famous Qāḍī ʿAbd al-Jabbār (AD 935–1025), whom Ibn ʿAbbād invited to Rayy and made Chief Qāḍī there.[161] The links between Muʿtazilism and Zaydism were close,[162] and the former exercised a particular influence on the development of Zaydī theology, which can neatly be characterized as Muʿtazilī.

Third, the Ṣaffārid court in Sijistān (Sīstān) – visited by al-Sijistānī, and presided over by its cultured ruler Abū Jaʿfar Aḥmad b. Muḥammad b. Khalaf b. al-Layth – was, despite its distance from Baghdad, clearly in the grip of a great cultural efflorescence, driven, it would seem, by the dynamo of Abū Jaʿfar's own intellectualism.[163] The early Ṣaffārids were associated with Khārijism and one of the founders of the dynasty was even accused of being an Ismāʿīlī.[164] However, 'the strength of Khārijism in Sīstān lay mainly in the small towns and villages of the countryside rather than in great centres of population.'[165] And by the time of al-Sijistānī's visits in the tenth century AD, the Ṣaffārid court was orthodox Sunnī.[166] But, as Kraemer points out, this did not impede a certain eclecticism from pervading the court milieu, and it is clear that Abū Jaʿfar's was not simply a court ruled by the orthodox *ʿulamāʾ*:

> Abū Jaʿfar presided over many of his court sessions with the erudite by posing questions, often along the lines of *questiones naturales.* He commented upon sayings of the ancients and upon Arab proverbs. His interests went beyond wisdom literature, for in one discussion he compares the philosophers of Islam to Socrates, Plato, and Aristotle, to the detriment, it may be added,

of the former. He was sufficiently informed to assess the relative merits of al-Kindī and Thābit b. Qurra.[167]

The Sāmānid court at Bukhārā, the last of the brief case studies of court, culture and religion which we will outline here, extended its patronage to al-ʿĀmirī who lived in Bukhārā in the latter part of his life.[168] The Sāmānids were Persian Sunnīs, but Ismāʿīlī doctrine had made a considerable impact on both rulers and ruled, and even a visitor like al-ʿĀmirī was suspected of adhering to this creed.[169] (Such suspicions do not seem to have been uncommon: as noted above, al-Tawḥīdī also is suspected of having had some kind of contact with Ismāʿīlism.) In its mixture then, of Sunnism and Ismāʿīlī heterodoxy, the Sāmānid court was typical of so many of the courts of the age: liberal, less than rigidly dogmatic, variously heterodox and perhaps, *as a direct result*, immensely cultured.[170] It is in itself a valuable paradigm for the Age of Fārābism which might with justification be usefully categorized by those same epithets.

This chapter has surveyed the undeniable association between court and culture and has stressed the eclectic and generally tolerant nature of so many of the courts. The following chapters will examine the epistemological substrate of some of the thought which was purveyed so freely in the courts and *majālis* of the rulers and their *wazīr*s; in particular, they will examine the epistemology of the five major thinkers who are the subject of this book.

2

THE EPISTEMOLOGICAL SUBSTRATE OF FĀRĀBISM (i): THE PARADIGM OF THE SECOND MASTER

The Quest for Knowledge

It has become almost a cliché when writing about medieval Islam, and in particular when describing the lengths to which such men as the collectors of Islamic tradition (*ḥadīth*) went to acquire their knowledge,[1] to stress the motif of 'travel in search of knowledge' (*riḥla fī ṭalab al-ʿilm*).[2] There was, as it were, a 'great tradition', not, of course, in the crude Leavisite literary sense,[3] but one which developed whereby scholars and students of diverse types and origins spent a large part of their early lives, at least, moving from one centre of learning to another and from one master or professor to the next. Such lust for acquiring the traditions or knowledge of the age was often combined with the pilgrimage to Mecca.[4] There is a certain analogy here to the 'grand tour' of Europe, undertaken in the west by youthful scions of wealthy or aristocratic families in the Age of the Enlightenment and afterwards, though it must be admitted that the motivations of the latter, even if nominally imbued by the impulse for education, may often have been somewhat inferior to those of their Muslim forebears.

The Prophet Muḥammad in a famous tradition had early articulated the notion that knowledge should be sought even as far as China. And his counsels were obeyed! The life of the great Muslim traditionist, Muḥammad b. Ismāʿīl al-Bukhārī (AD 810–70), perhaps the most revered and famed of all the Muslim collectors of tradition with his renowned compilation of *ḥadīth* entitled the *Ṣaḥīḥ* (the *True* or the *Authentic*), presents a typical early example of the paradigm: starting his study of traditions at the age of ten, he went on pilgrimage to Mecca when he was sixteen and later roamed the Islamic world 'from Khurāsān to Egypt' studying, learning and collecting traditions.[5] The life of the Maghribī traveller, Ibn Baṭṭūṭa, to whom we have earlier referred, presents a typical later example from a generation several centuries removed from that of al-Bukhārī, in which the impulse to travel combined with the pilgrimage to Mecca and the thirst for knowledge became formalized or canonized in the *riḥla* genre.[6] It is this latter genre which may be described as the formal response to, or articulation of, Muḥammad's earlier injunction to travel even as far as China in search of knowledge.

Of course, the experiences undergone and the knowledge laboriously sought and happily acquired, were by no means monolithic: the Islamic Middle Ages (and indeed beyond) witnessed a search by multifarious scholars for much more than just traditions from or concerning the founder Prophet Muḥammad. There were different categories of knowledge to be gained which might, indeed, include the collection, establishment and authentication of traditions, but which also embraced historical knowledge, philosophical knowledge, theological knowledge, and knowledge that was esoteric or mystical to name but a few other types.[7] Philosophical knowledge was clearly of a somewhat different order from traditional knowledge, but each had the potential and capacity to produce an individual theory of knowledge or epistemology. Sensory or experiential knowledge was by no means eschewed, and thus a Muslim thinker need not feel obliged to share with Plato the latter's distrust and rejection of knowledge gleaned by the senses.[8] Scripture itself, as with the Ismāʿīlī branch of Shīʿite Islam, could be the jealous custodian or depository of a secret, esoteric (*bāṭin*) core of knowledge where the mysteries of the Qur'ān, and interpretation thereof, could only be detected or unlocked by an educated initiate, imposing in consequence a placid acceptance of the superficial obvious (*ẓāhir*) sense of scripture on those lacking the necessary knowledge. With such groups, real knowledge became the gnostic province of a privileged and specialized few.

A reshaped or revamped philosophical tool or method could often be reborn from the coils of an outworn or antique epistemology, or final acknowledgement that the old objects of knowledge themselves were no longer adequate or even valid. For example, Lenn and Madeleine Goodman have noted:

> Emanation was perfected by the neo-Platonists, quite consciously as an alternative to creation because the learned neo-Platonic philosophers did not choose to redescend into the

> anthropomorphic cosmogonies from which Aristotle had rescued them with great difficulty only a few centuries earlier.[9]

In that emanation was an attempt to help men understand the relationship between – or, at least, the *possibility* of a relationship between – the transcendent and the corporeal, it may usefully (if loosely) be classified here as an epistemological tool as well as one embraced by Neoplatonic philosophy and theology. As such, it had a dynamic and widespread applicability in the history of the development of Islamic thought and philosophy.

A final example of the multifarious nature of knowledge, and the objects and tools of such knowledge in medieval Islam, lies in its mystical aspect and, in particular, the usages by varying constituencies of the two Arabic words *ʿilm* and *maʿrifa*, both of which mean 'knowledge'. These have been clearly surveyed by Franz Rosenthal: he notes that early on *ʿilm* meant 'religious knowledge in the legal-traditionalist sense'[10] and that, in general, Islamic mysticism – ṣūfism – was happy to adopt and absorb the term, though perhaps with some refinements. *Maʿrifa*, in its technical sense, was used to refer to (gnostic) knowledge 'about God, [and] was in all likelihood shared originally by Ṣûfîs with other Muslim religious thinkers who found the essential basis of faith in the knowledge about God in the first place and, thereafter, in the knowledge about a varying number of religious beliefs'.[11] It seems that at first 'there was no real difference between *maʿrifah* and *ʿilm* at the earliest stages of Muslim metaphysical thought, and the same would seem to be valid for mysticism'.[12] Later, however, despite the continued usage of *ʿilm* and the fact that some mystical authors placed this kind of knowledge above *maʿrifa*, the latter became 'a term expressive of the distinctive essence of mysticism'.[13] Later too, gnostic knowledge (*maʿrifa*) became the preserve of the saints alone.[14]

Knowledge, then, was diverse and multifaceted. The words which in Arabic indicated knowledge were by no means monovalent or monolithic but often culturally and temporally conditioned and capable of a variety of senses. In this chapter, and those that follow, we will ask some of the following questions about the five thinkers who constitute the subject matter of this book: What was the nature of the knowledge which they sought and acquired? What were their epistemological preoccupations? Can we identify a Neoplatonic substrate lurking beneath the thought of some or all of them? How did their ethics and their politics interact? In conclusion, we will try to see if it is possible to posit or formulate some kind of general theory of epistemology, or at least the principles upon which the thought of Fārābism might be said to be based. In other words, what do we mean when we talk about the epistemology of Fārābism?

Al-Fārābī and Knowledge

What is knowledge? What can man know and how can he know it? Numerous answers have been given down the ages and numerous aspects of the same problem have been surveyed at various times. One remembers the great nominalist debate in medieval Europe[15] and the discussion of the concept of universals has continued into modern times.[16] A.J. Ayer's logical positivism with its verification principle provides one twentieth-century response to the problem of how to evaluate knowledge and what may validly be evaluated.[17] The nature, concerns and problems of epistemology in any age are huge and the answers provided by thinkers and philosophers have been commensurately vast. Only a few selective references, examples and definitions will be provided here by way of illustration. David Pears identifies, for instance, three divisions of knowledge: 'Factual knowledge, knowing how to do things and acquaintance'.[18] A further, overlapping triad is cited: 'perceptual knowledge, knowledge of universals and memory of past facts which [the person] himself had perceived'.[19] He concludes with a question which may be asked of every epistemologist and, indeed, of each of the thinkers examined in this book: 'Is the philosopher's task merely to describe the structure of human knowledge, and perhaps to fix its limits, or is it also to produce a rational reconstruction of the whole thing, which would exhibit the true relations between its parts?'[20]

Epistemology itself, as a term, has been defined as 'the branch of philosophy concerned with the theory of knowledge. Traditionally, central issues in epistemology are the nature and derivation of knowledge, the scope of knowledge, and the reliability of claims to knowledge.'[21] This brief but useful definition is fleshed out in greater depth by O'Connor and Carr:

> Epistemology, the theory of knowledge, is concerned with knowledge in a number of ways. First and foremost it seeks to give an account of the nature of *knowing* in general.... A second concern of epistemology is with the *sources* of knowledge, with the investigation of the nature and variety of *modes of acquiring*

> knowledge.... The third concern, with the *scope* of knowledge, is clearly closely related to the other two.... The fourth concern of epistemology has been, and for many still is, to defend our criteria for knowledge against the attack of *scepticism*.[22]

The focus upon epistemology in its multifarious forms was equally intense in medieval Islam and bears comparison with developments in medieval Europe. Details may, of course, have varied, but the broad concentration on knowledge, frequently divine, sometimes secular, usually legalistic, makes an epistemological assessment of the Islamic scene both profoundly difficult and, paradoxically, structurally possible: it is difficult because of the huge quantity of material to be surveyed and assessed. Fortunately for the student and scholar of Islamic studies, an excellent introduction to the field has already been undertaken by Franz Rosenthal in his magisterial book *Knowledge Triumphant*. The task is made, at the same time, if not easier, at least structurally possible in view of the similarity of the epistemological preoccupations of many of the Islamic philosophers, thinkers, and theologians. In other words, the same problems often arose in the Islamic world as they did in ancient and medieval Europe, and scholars might either agree with, or *react* in full knowledge against, their predecessors. A brief example must suffice here: Plato's scepticism about knowledge derived from sensory perception is a philosophical cliché; we have alluded to it earlier.[23] Some Muslim philosophers, however, like the medieval Brethren of Purity (Ikhwān al-Ṣafā'), felt free, having clearly considered the same problem, to react against Plato (whose views they seem in some other things, especially the veneration of Socrates, to have admired) and to produce an epistemology in which 'some knowledge of the divine could be acquired here in this world as a means of achieving Paradise'.[24] In a commentary on the Platonic dictum that 'knowledge is remembrance', the Brethren of Purity insisted on interpreting it to mean that

> the soul is 'potentially knowledgeable' (*ʿallāma bi 'l-quwwa*) and needs instruction to become 'actually knowledgeable' (*ʿallāma bi 'l-fiʿl*). They explain carefully that the method of instruction should be through the senses, then by the intellect and finally by logical deduction; but without the senses man can know nothing.[25]

In view of the way in which Islamic philosophers often invoked the authority of Plato, Aristotle and Plotinus, often creating in the process an Islamic Platonism, Aristotelianism and Neoplatonism, it is not surprising that the epistemologies which underlay these three broad 'schools of philosophy' should have influenced so many of the major and minor thinkers in the Islamic east, and at least have been reflected upon by others before ultimate rejection. The passion for classification, for example, which imbued so much of Aristotelian epistemology, was seized upon by al-Fārābī; and he is the kernel and primary focal point of this book whose task is to analyse and survey the broad doctrine of Fārābism in its epistemological aspects.

Since this volume attempts only to provide an introduction to a massive field, the approach of this chapter and its successor, for the most part, will be confined to two very basic epistemological questions: *What* can be known? *How* can it be known? In other words, to refer back to O'Connor and Carr's classification cited above, we will concentrate mainly on the *scope* and *sources* of knowledge, and second, on the *modes of acquiring* that knowledge.[26] Other aspects of epistemology will not thereby be totally ignored or eschewed, but they will be referred to where necessary in passing. Though we will not, in general, discuss the concept of scepticism with reference to the five thinkers under discussion in this book, we may, however, note that such an approach could in some senses be seen as a logical theological successor or counterpart to the *via negativa* espoused by some of the theologians.[27] They, like the philosophers and specialists in logic and like the jurists, were profoundly influenced by epistemological discussion which 'penetrated right to the core of Muslim thinking'.[28]

Al-Fārābī's own epistemology can by no means be restricted to, or structured upon, some narrow medieval quadrivium. He himself provides a clue to its breadth in his statement that 'Wisdom is knowledge of the remote causes'.[29] However, in an attempt to provide a manageable framework within which to consider the scope of al-Fārābī's knowledge and its sources, it is proposed here to utilize the bibliographical frame presented by Nicholas Rescher: under the heading 'Theory of Knowledge', he cites five Arabic works either by or attributed to al-Fārābī.[30] In what follows here it is proposed to survey the content of the first three which are definitely of Fārābian provenance (the survey will not, however, follow the order in which Rescher itemizes them). These are the vital and primary sources of al-Fārābī's own epistemology. Their titles are:

1 *The Book of the Enumeration of the Sciences* (*Kitāb Iḥṣā' al-ʿUlūm*)
2 *Epistle on the Intellect* (*Risāla fī 'l-ʿAql*)

3 *The Book of Letters* (*Kitāb al-Ḥurūf*) (with Muhsin Mahdi, I have preferred the latter, apparently older, title to the longer *Book of Words and Letters* (*Kitāb al-Alfāẓ wa 'l-Ḥurūf*) itemized by Rescher)[31]

Reference will also be made in the survey and discussion that follows to a fourth work: *The Book of Indication of the Path of Happiness* (*Kitāb al-Tanbīh ʿalā Sabīl al-Saʿāda*).

It has been well emphasized that Greek logic became the heart and basis of Islamic epistemology from the ninth century onwards.[32] It provided 'the only systematic scientific framework available to Muslim scholars for intellectual expression from that time'. Logic was a science (*ʿilm*) which resulted in 'certain knowledge (*al-ʿilm al-yaqīn*)' but logic also 'provided the justification and the system of classification for scholarly and scientific disciplines'.[33] All this was as true of al-Fārābī as of his philosophical successors. He had an immense veneration for logic and this is apparent in his *Enumeration of the Sciences*.[34] Not only did the logician, who depended on Greek forms of logic, incur the suspicion and wrath of some of the theologians,[35] but the hostility of some of the grammarians as well. It is clear that al-Fārābī's veneration and respect for logic had an impact, not only on the actual content of his metaphysics and philosophy but also on his theoretical classification of the subject matter of knowledge itself. In other words, logic had a profound epistemological dimension in both the thought and the classification of al-Fārābī. Al-Rabe believes that al-Fārābī gave a prime place to logic in his *Enumeration of the Sciences*, devoting the second chapter (*Faṣl*) to this subject, because he specifically wished to defend that science against the onslaught of the grammarians.[36]

Bearing all these remarks in mind then, we may turn now to a more thorough survey of the contents of that work of al-Fārābī's, *The Enumeration of the Sciences*, as a first illustration of *what* al-Fārābī believed could be known, and the scope and sources of that knowledge. Al-Rabe maintains that the way in which al-Fārābī classified the sciences in this book was in no way arbitrary but was carefully structured and thought out, deliberately giving a prime place to logic.[37] In the former's view, the philosopher's classification reflects a specific philosophical approach and viewpoint;[38] and, if only by virtue of its being the earliest known Arabic-Islamic classification of scientific knowledge, albeit a very distinguished and distinctive example, it provided a powerful paradigm for all those Muslim classifications in their various forms which followed.[39] It was also clearly admired in medieval Europe, where it was translated twice into Latin in the twelfth century (by John of Seville and Gerard of Cremona) as well as into the Spanish and Hebrew languages.[40]

Al-Fārābī articulated his intention in writing *The Enumeration of the Sciences* as follows:

> Our intention in this book is to enumerate the sciences (*al-ʿulūm*) actually acknowledged to be science[s]. We will apprise [the reader] of everything that each of them contains, their constituent parts and the composition of each of these parts.[41]

By undertaking such a classification, it is al-Fārābī's intention to help his reader in what may be separated into five different ways; these may be characterized as the five epistemological goals of the whole undertaking:

1. The reader – whom al-Fārābī calls here simply *al-insān*, that is, 'the human being', 'the man', perhaps thereby wishing to stress the maximum utility and appeal of his classification – can evaluate properly what he wishes to study with real insight and knowledge;
2. He can draw comparisons between the various sciences in terms of their relative merits or profitability;
3. He can use the classification to lay bare false claims to knowledge by others;
4. Likewise, the classification can aid in the examination of the actual breadth or otherwise of someone's knowledge in a science;
5. The versatile autodidact (*al-muta'addib*) and would-be scholar can profitably use the classification in al-Fārābī's book as an introduction to the sciences which he wishes to study.[42]

These five epistemological goals of al-Fārābī's classification may neatly be encapsulated in five key words: evaluative, comparative, detective, interrogative and autodidactic.

In his *Enumeration of the Sciences*, al-Fārābī eschewed a division of knowledge in general into theological and philosophical sciences, unlike al-Ghazālī (AD 1058–1111) and later Ibn Khaldūn (AD 1332–1406),[43] and preferred instead in *this* work to organize his classification into the following five chapters or sections (*Fuṣūl*): here is al-Fārābī's thumbnail sketch of *what* can be known, to a greater or lesser degree:

1 Chapter 1: The Science of Language (*al-Faṣl al-Awwal fī ʿIlm al-Lisān*)
2 Chapter 2: The Science of Logic (*al-Faṣl al-Thānī fī ʿIlm al-Manṭiq*)
3 Chapter 3: The Mathematical Sciences (lit. The Formative Science) (*al-Faṣl al-Thālith fī ʿIlm al-Taʿālīm*)
4 Chapter 4: Physics and Metaphysics (*al-Faṣl al-Rābiʿ fī 'l-ʿIlm al-Tabīʿī wa 'l-ʿIlm al-Ilāhī*)
5 Chapter 5: Civil Science,[44] Jurisprudence and Scholastic Theology (*al-Faṣl al-Khāmis fī 'l-ʿIlm al-Madanī wa ʿIlm al-Fiqh wa ʿIlm al-Kalām*)

Here then, we find eight major headings under which knowledge may be classified. There is a clear Aristotelian stress on the primacy of logic, whose study, together with that of language, is required *before* embarking on the other sciences.[45] This is very much in accord with the Greek legacy bequeathed to Islamic epistemology, which we have already noted.

Al-Fārābī's principal subject headings are further subdivided: the Mathematical Sciences, for example, comprise no neat or concise medieval quadrivium of Arithmetic, Geometry, Astronomy and Music but an extended sevenfold classification into Arithmetic (*ʿIlm al-ʿAdad*), Geometry (*ʿIlm al-Handasa*), Optics (*ʿIlm al-Manāẓir*), Astronomy (*ʿIlm al-Nujūm*), Music (*ʿIlm al-Mūsīqā*), Weights (*ʿIlm al-Athqāl*) and Mechanical Artifices[46] (*ʿIlm al-Ḥiyal*). These divisions are themselves further subdivided, a popular example of this being into the applied or practical (*al-ʿamalī*) and the theoretical (*al-naẓarī*)[47] aspects of the subject.

Physics is a science which examines those things that are corporeal (*al-ajsām al-ṭabīʿiyya*) and their accidents (*al-aʿrāḍ*), and is underpinned by the Aristotelian doctrine of the four causes: material, formal, efficient and final.[48] The ensuing eightfold subdivision is also deeply Aristotelian:[49] the science of Physics may be divided as follows: the examination of basic physical principles; the examination of the whole nature and number of simple corporeal elements (*al-ajsām al-basīṭa*); the examination of physical generation and corruption; the examination of the principles of accidents (*al-aʿrāḍ*); the examination of complex or compound bodies formed from the basic elements (*al-ajsām al-murakkaba ʿan al-isṭaqisāt*); the examination of mineralogy; the examination of botany; and, finally, the examination of zoology. The latter, presumably, here embraces mankind as well as the rest of the animal kingdom, since reference is made to both a *Book of Animals* and a *Book of the Soul* or, to use more Aristotelian-like titles, to a *Historia Animalium* as well as to a *De Anima*.[50]

Third, as a final example of al-Fārābī's penchant for subdividing and elaborating the principal eightfold epistemological division of his *Enumeration of the Sciences*, there is the following subdivision of Metaphysics: this science, he says, firstly enquires into beings (*al-mawjūdāt*) and their fundamental ontological characteristics; second, it looks into the principles of proof or demonstration in individual theoretical sciences; and third, it examines beings which are neither corporeal (*al-mawjūdāt allatī laysat bi-ajsām*), nor in other bodies, and this examination ends in or at the study of God Himself, who is described here in a characteristically negative fashion by al-Fārābī.[51]

The above brief survey of the content, classification and subclassifications of al-Fārābī's *Enumeration of the Sciences* provides a first response to the question as to *what* sorts of thing al-Fārābī believed one could have some kind of knowledge about, even if it were only partial or negative. If we now ask about the scope and sources of that knowledge, the answers are not difficult to find: the scope is wide, embraces that which is corporeal and non-corporeal, and includes much that Aristotle himself found necessary to survey and include in his own vast *oeuvre*. Indeed, the long shadow of Aristotle hangs over much of what has been surveyed above, and over the whole of al-Fārābī's epistemology: we have noted his terminology of accidents and causes; we have seen the impact of his own classificatory systems; and we note in passing that many of al-Fārābī's chapter headings or numerous subdivisions, itemized above, directly parallel or at the very least echo works by Aristotle or attributed to the Stagirite (these range from the already mentioned *De Anima* and *Historia Animalium*, through the *Metaphysica* and the *De Generatione et Corruptione*, to the spurious *De Plantis*.[52]

Al-Fārābī's epistemology then, at least from the point of view of what can be known, and its scope and sources, is Greek Aristotelian through and through – or so we might conclude from the above. But there is another side to the epistemological coin which must not be ignored here, and which al-Fārābī, in *The Enumeration of the Sciences*, himself does not ignore: the Neoplatonic dimension. This is articulated or epitomized in a negative vocabulary which signals a dimension of knowledge where one records, paradoxically, what *cannot* be known and cannot be truly articulated except in negatives. It is a truism that a reference to the existence of a branch of knowledge need not in any way imply the least real understanding of that knowledge.

This is as true of Fārābian epistemology as elsewhere. Al-Fārābī is aware of the limitations of both positive epistemology and language itself: as we have noted, he proclaims that the third major area of enquiry in Metaphysics ends 'at a Perfect (*Kāmil*) whom none can surpass in perfection'. He has neither peer nor opposite, neither predecessor nor antecedent, and owes His existence to no one else and nothing else.[53]

The basic conclusions from the above, thus far, must be that Fārābist epistemology is built upon the twin foundations of Aristotelian 'positivism' and Neoplatonic negativism. How far, it may be asked, is this true of his other epistemological works in particular (especially those others which were earlier chosen for survey), and for the whole of the epistemology behind Fārābism, in general? An attempt will be made to answer the first part of this question now; an answer to the second will become apparent later in this book.

First, however, we might profitably note with al-Rabe,[54] that al-Fārābī appears to have established, if not a rival, at least a parallel scheme of basic classification in another of his works to which we have already alluded, *The Book of Indication of the Path of Happiness.* Here philosophy is subdivided into the theoretical and the practical[55] and then there are further subdivisions: for example, theoretical philosophy embraces the Mathematical Sciences (*ʿIlm al-Taʿālīm*), Physics (*al-ʿIlm al-Ṭabīʿī*), and Metaphysics (*ʿIlm mā Baʿd al-Ṭabīʿiyyāt*).[56] In effect, this parallels chapters 3 and 4 of *The Enumeration of the Sciences.*[57] The alternative division here, in this *Book of Indication of the Path of Happiness*, into the theoretical and the practical is an interesting and intriguing one in the Fārābian corpus.[58] It is true that he did not make it an important aspect of his *Enumeration of the Sciences*, although the two words certainly appear, as we have already noted. However, it is a significant epistemological division in *The Book of Indication of the Path of Happiness* and must, therefore, be borne in mind, alongside the classification in *The Enumeration of the Sciences*, whenever any *overall* survey or assessment of al-Fārābī's epistemology or classificatory apparatus is attempted. And for al-Fārābī, the meanings of these two key words 'theoretical' and 'practical' are very easy. They are neatly described in *The Book of Indication* in an almost simplistic fashion: theoretical knowledge is that which, if known, does not engender or require action. For example, one does not feel obliged to *act* on the knowledge of God's unity or the createdness of the world. However, practical knowledge does precipitate action.[59]

If we turn now to the second of the three major epistemological works earlier suggested for survey,[60] al-Fārābī's important *Epistle on the Intellect*, we perceive here in operation a quite different structure. This work is, of course, shorter than *The Enumeration of the Sciences* but it is also not intended to be a formal classification of knowledge like the latter. None the less, it has a considerable epistemological significance both in terms of its structure and content for any study of al-Fārābī, and for this reason it will be surveyed here. Greater emphasis will be placed in what immediately follows on the *structure* of the *Epistle*; while the *content* will be drawn upon in more detail when we come to an analysis of *how* one can know in Fārābian thought. This will, of course, involve a survey of al-Fārābī's complex theory of intellection.

Jolivet has noted how the Athenian School, in situating the noetic between physics and metaphysics, signalled, from an epistemological perspective, the singular status of the intellect.[61] I have stressed elsewhere how the ten intellects emanating from God in al-Fārābī's classical and elaborate emanationist hierarchy – and, in particular, the Tenth Agent or Active Intellect – act as a bridge between transcendence and corporeality.[62] In other words, intellect, and thus the whole discussion of knowledge of whatever kind and however achieved, has an ontological as well as an epistemological function and dimension. It was one of the fruits of Neoplatonism that the intellect gained a prominent ontological rank.[63] Indeed, Jolivet holds that al-Fārābī turns Aristotelian epistemology into metaphysics.[64] The noetic inherited by al-Fārābī is both the result of a long tradition and also a crossroads.[65] These few points should be borne in mind as background to the survey that follows.

Al-Fārābī's *Epistle on the Intellect* is not, we stressed above, intended to be a formal classification of the whole sphere of knowledge in the manner of his *Enumeration of the Sciences*. However, the former could usefully be defined as a species of extended encyclopaedia or dictionary article,[66] very neatly organized, encapsulating the numerous senses of the single Arabic word *ʿAql* (intellect), a word whose diverse meanings are immediately recognized by al-Fārābī himself in the opening lines of his *Epistle*: 'The noun "intellect" has diverse senses' (*Ism al-ʿaql yuqāl ʿalā anḥā' kathīra*).[67] He then goes on to list what are for him the six principal usages of the word.[68] The *Epistle* proceeds immediately to discuss and analyse each of these in turn and this discussion and analysis occupy the rest of the *Epistle*. However, equal weight is not given to each of the six definitions of 'intellect': those which appear in the initial list of al-Fārābī as first, second, third, fourth and sixth are each covered in the body of the text by two to three pages each.[69] However, al-Fārābī's fifth definition of intellect – 'The intellect which he [Aristotle] mentions in the *De Anima* (lit. *Book of the Soul*)' (*Al-ʿaql alladhī yadhkuruhu fī Kitāb al-Nafs*)[70] – receives a much more extensive coverage,[71] being itself divided into four major subsections: Potential Intellect (*ʿaql bi 'l-quwwa*); Actual Intellect (*ʿaql bi 'l-fiʿl*); Acquired Intellect (*ʿaql mustafād*); and Agent Intellect (*al-ʿaql al-faʿʿāl*).[72]

What is interesting in his enumeration of the six major senses of 'intellect' is that al-Fārābī deliberately links four of them to – and underpins them by – references to specific Aristotelian works, where it is claimed that Aristotle mentions that particular type of intellect: *The Posterior Analytics* (*Kitāb al-Burhān*) (Intellect no. 3); *The Ethics* (*Kitāb al-Akhlāq*) (Intellect no. 4); *De Anima* (*Kitāb al-Nafs*) (Intellect no. 5); and *The Metaphysics* (*Kitāb mā Baʿd al-Ṭabīʿa*) (Intellect no. 6).[73]

This brief survey of al-Fārābī's *Epistle on the Intellect*, which elaborates *what* can be known about the single word 'intellect' under six major headings or definitions, also elaborates in part the *scope* and *sources* of that work. The first is paradoxically both narrow and broad at the same time, concentrating as it does on the precise articulation and definition of a single word and yet showing all too clearly the multifaceted dimensions of that word in the world of human understanding and epistemology. The second, the sources, are clearly Aristotelian in inspiration through and through and declare a precise and joyful dependence on the 'First Master'. There are, however, Neoplatonic aspects as well. As with much of al-Fārābī's writing, the signs of the latter are never far away. For example, form is emanated to the inhabitants of the sublunary world by the Active or Agent Intellect, an adaptation, albeit a Neoplatonic one, of Plotinus' doctrine of the emanation of form by the Universal Soul.[74]

The epistemological conclusions to be drawn from the *Epistle on the Intellect* are clear: like *The Enumeration of the Sciences*, this *Epistle* is underpinned by a substrate of both Aristotelianism and Neoplatonism. As in some of his other works which are not to be classified directly under the heading of epistemology, these two philosophies stand shoulder to shoulder and frequently interact. Philosophically, this must be accounted a major facet of al-Fārābī's philosophy and metaphysics; epistemologically the combination is intriguing because of the concepts of hierarchy and emanation which are infiltrated into the basic Aristotelian data and terminology, and also because of the attempt, noted earlier, to view epistemology in terms of ontology.

The role of the Tenth Intellect – the Active or Agent Intellect – with its paramount position among the six intellects referred to above, yet its lower hierarchical position as only tenth in al-Fārābī's emanationist scheme, and its activity as an 'ontological bridge', is a striking illustration of all this.

Can we make the same statements of the third of the three epistemological works earlier selected for particular study, *The Book of Letters*? Is this work also built upon a foundation of Aristotelianism and Neoplatonism which have a direct bearing on the epistemology of al-Fārābī?

The most cursory examination shows that here it is the former, rather than the latter, which plays the predominant role in underpinning the content of *The Book of Letters*. This is by no means a handbook of Neoplatonic emanation but a work which is clearly and consciously modelled upon Aristotle's *Metaphysics*. Yet there is no blind or slavish rigidity or devotion in the way in which the 'Second Master', al-Fārābī, chooses to follow the 'First Master', Aristotle. The former has felt free to change the latter's arrangement in the *Metaphysics*, and, moreover, to introduce and develop new materials of relevance to translation theory, linguistics, theology and philosophy.[75] Mahdi notes that the intention of al-Fārābī is 'the examination of "in how many ways" a thing is said to be'.[76] This is clearly in accordance with Aristotle who, at the beginning of Book Gamma of the *Metaphysics*, proclaims: 'There is a discipline which studies that which is *qua* thing-that-is and those things that hold good of this in its own right.... That which *is* may be so called in several ways.'[77] Kirwan points out in this translation that '"Discipline" translates "*epistēmē*", traditionally rendered "knowledge"';[78] and there is no doubt that in both the work of Aristotle and that of al-Fārābī, the study of being and the quiddity of things has a profound epistemological dimension.

This is highlighted in al-Fārābī's *Book of Letters* by an examination of the basic structure of the work, which has already been carefully and neatly analysed and divided up by Muhsin Mahdi.[79] Mahdi shows that the *Book of Letters* falls usefully into three major divisions:

1 The Particles [or Letters] and the Names of the [Aristotelian] Categories (*al-Ḥurūf wa Asmā' al-Maqūlāt*);
2 The Phenomenon of Words, Philosophy and Religion (*Ḥudūth al-Alfāẓ wa 'l-Falsafa wa 'l-Milla*); and
3 The Particles of Interrogation (*Ḥurūf al-Su'āl*).[80]

The first division, inescapably Aristotelian in orientation, considers

Arabic particles representing being (*ḥarf inna*) and time (*ḥarf matā*) before surveying and analysing the other Categories, together with some related but separate topics. The second division moves away somewhat from Aristotle's *Metaphysics* to survey in some depth such subjects as the relationships and contacts between philosophy and religion; the phenomenon of letters and words in a community; the origin of a community's language: and the coining (*ikhtirāʿ*) and translation of names. The third division moves a little closer to the Aristotelian paradigm again with its survey and analysis of types of discourse and interrogative particles like 'What?' (*mā*), 'How?' (*kayf*), and others.[81]

From these three divisions, two particular passages stand out which have interesting epistemological dimensions with regard to the question of *what* may be known. First, in the premier division identified and isolated by Mahdi, al-Fārābī talks *inter alia* of *The Primary Subjects of the Arts and the Sciences* (*al-Mawḍūʿāt al-Uwal* [*sic*] *li'l-Ṣanāʾiʿ wa 'l-ʿUlūm*): reference is made in what follows to Logic, Physics, Civil Science, Mathematical Science and Metaphysics.[82] Here, at least, there is some harmony with what was classified in *The Enumeration of the Sciences*,[83] though the match is by no means total and other subjects are introduced as well.[84] Comparisons may also be made with the classification identified earlier in *The Book of Indication of the Path of Happiness*, particularly with regard to the latter's division of knowledge into the theoretical and the practical, a division also present in *The Book of Letters*.[85]

Second, in his analysis of the interrogative particle 'What?' (*ḥarf mā*), al-Fārābī points to the range of ways in which the question 'What?' can be employed to elicit either a simple or more complex and precise response and piece of information.[86] The particle 'What?' is thus an epistemological trigger which can be used both to derive a simple identification by name of some object or person before one,[87] as well as the more sophisticated and precise type of information provided in response to a question such as 'What is that animal which is in India?'[88] The whole discussion here shows al-Fārābī's profound appreciation of language and the epistemological subtleties of its usage, as well as its interaction with such fields as perception and psychology. Behind it – or perhaps better, beyond it – lie questions of education and its various levels, knowledge versus ignorance, as well as al-Fārābī's complex theory of intellection to which we will presently come. For al-Fārābī's perfect epistemological paradigm is that in which the Being who knows (*al-ʿĀqil*), the intellect (*al-ʿAql*) and the intelligible or that which is known or comprehended (*al-Maʿqūl*) are merged indissolubly and ineluctably in the One who is, of course, God Himself.[89] In semiotic terms, al-Fārābī's *Book of Letters* signals a paradigm of imperfect intellection, mediated through the channels of a fundamental Aristotelian terminology, whose secular multiplicity contrasts sharply with the perfect unity of Knower and Knowledge in the Deity.

So far we have concentrated on trying to provide some answers to the question of *what* kinds of things and subjects al-Fārābī believed could be known, in some way. In the process we have surveyed three of his principal works which may fairly be labelled epistemological in orientation and content, if not always or necessarily in overt intention. This chapter turns now to the second question of *how* al-Fārābī believed knowledge could be attained. The key to this is an examination of al-Fārābī's theory of intellection.

The complexities of this theory may be somewhat alleviated if we follow first of all al-Fārābī's own *sixfold* division of reason (*ʿaql*), as outlined in his key *Epistle on the Intellect*. As we have already noted, al-Fārābī's basic intention is to enumerate the various senses of the word 'intellect' or 'reason'.

The *first* major type of reason or intellect is that by virtue of which the ordinary people (*al-jumhūr*) characterize a human being as rational or intelligent (*ʿāqil*). The key Arabic word used here for this type of intellect is *taʿaqqul*, which may be translated as 'prudence', 'discernment', 'understanding' or 'judiciousness'. As Fakhry stresses, al-Fārābī infuses this Arabic word with the sense of Aristotelian *phrónēsis*, a Greek word which may be rendered as 'prudence' or 'thoughtfulness'. Generally speaking, the faculty of *taʿaqqul* is a characteristic of he who acts for the good (*man kāna fāḍilan*). The word thus has at least two principal facets, and Badawī has noted an overlap between the sense of 'prudence', which it bears here, and the sense of the fourth type of Fārābian intellect, which we will shortly consider, namely moral prudence.[90]

The *second* major kind of intellect or reason in al-Fārābī's list is that which the scholastic theologians or dialecticians (*al-mutakallimūn*) present as having a proscriptive or prescriptive function, a negative dismissive or a positive affirmative quality. There is an immediacy of recognition or obviousness associated with this intellect. Fakhry describes it as that 'which is in part identical with common sense'.[91]

The *third* of al-Fārābī's intellects may loosely be described as natural perception. He finds its source in Aristotle's *Posterior Analytics* (*Kitāb al-Burhān*): it is the faculty of the soul which enables man to grasp the certainty (*al-yaqīn*) of some basic universal and necessary true principles. The faculty derives not from analogy or logical skills or thought but from one's own nature or, at the very least, arises in one's youth. It appears then that it is either inborn or acquired very early in life. Man is ignorant of from where and how this reason comes. Fakhry neatly describes this reason as 'the faculty of perceiving the primary principles of demonstration, instinctively and intuitively' and al-Fārābī tells us that it is a part of the soul (*juz' mā min al-nafs*).[92]

The *fourth* in this sixfold division of intellects is, loosely, al-Fārābī's *developed* voice of conscience. He finds it in Book Six of Aristotle's (*Nicomachean*) *Ethics* (*Kitāb al-Akhlāq*) and, as we have already noted, this quality of moral prudence (to use the term in Badawī's *Histoire de la Philosophie en Islam*), by which one knows good from evil, has a certain overlap with the prudence associated with the first kind of intellect discussed above. Once again, this intellect forms part of the soul; it is a faculty which derives from long experience.[93]

The *fifth* of the Fārābian intellects is at once the most important and the most complex of the six. It is the one that occupies most space in the philosopher's *Epistle on the Intellect*, and he divides it into four different types, finding his source once again in Aristotle, this time in the *De Anima*:

1 Potential Intellect (*ʿAql bi 'l-Quwwa*)
2 Actual Intellect (*ʿAql bi 'l-Fiʿl*)
3 Acquired Intellect (*ʿAql Mustafād*)
4 Agent or Active Intellect (*al-ʿAql al-Faʿʿāl*)[94]

Each of these intellects will be briefly described here:

Potential Intellect This is the reason or intellect which has the potential or capacity, in Fakhry's words, 'of abstracting the forms of existing entities with which it is ultimately identified'.[95] Potential Intellect thus becomes Actual Intellect. As al-Fārābī himself puts it:

> The intellect which is in potentiality is some soul, or part of a soul, or one of the faculties of the soul, or something whose essence is ready and prepared to abstract the quiddities of all existing things and their forms from their matters, so that it

makes all of them a form for itself or forms for itself. And those forms which are abstracted from their matters do not become abstracted from their matters in which their existence is unless they become forms for this essence [the intellect in potentiality]. Those forms abstracted from their matters which become forms in this essence are the intelligibles, and this name [intelligibles] is derived for them from the name of that essence which abstracts the forms of existing things, so that they become forms for it. That essence is like matter in which forms come to be. Now, if you imagine some corporeal matter, for example, a piece of wax on which an impression is stamped, and that impression and that form comes to be in its surface and its depth and that form gets possession of all of matter so that the matter in its complete totality becomes that form because the form is spread out in it – then your imagination is close to picturing the manner in which the forms of things come to be in that essence which is like matter and substratum for that form.[96]

Actual Intellect Fakhry notes that here 'the intelligibles in act (or forms) acquire a new mode of being ... the intelligibles in act, which are identical with the intellect in act, might be said to have become the subjects of active thought and not merely its objects'.[97] Al-Fārābī describes this intellect thus:

In accordance with [what has been said earlier about the Potential Intellect], you must imagine the coming to be of the forms of existing things [*al-mawjūdāt*] in that essence which Aristotle in the *De Anima* calls intellect in potentiality. And as long as there is not within it any of the forms of existing things, it is intellect in potentiality. However, when there come to be in it the forms of existing things, in accordance with the example which we have mentioned, then that essence becomes intellect in actuality. *This is the meaning of intellect in actuality.* And when there come to be in it the intelligibles which it abstracts from the matters, then those intelligibles become intelligibles in actuality.[98]

Acquired Intellect The above-mentioned Actual Intellect is clearly associated with the *mawjūdāt* which Hyman translates, as we have seen above, as 'existing things'. However, it is clear that the

Acquired Intellect operates on a more abstract level, or within a more abstract province. As one author puts it: 'Once the intellect becomes capable of comprehending abstractions, it is raised again to a higher level, that of the acquired intellect, or the level where human intellect becomes disposed to conceive abstract forms which have no connection with matter.'[99] Or, to put it a different way, the Acquired Intellect, in its relationship to the Actual Intellect, is:

> the agent of actualization to what is actualized. Moreover it differs from it in that the subject matter of its apprehension is the intelligible in act only. To this category belong intelligibles abstracted from matter by the former Reason, as well as the immaterial forms which this acquired Reason apprehends immediately, in the same way that it apprehends itself qua immaterial.[100]

Al-Fārābī notes: 'When the intellect in actuality thinks the intelligibles which are forms in it, in so far as they are intelligibles in actuality, then the intellect of which it was first said that it is the intellect in actuality, becomes now the acquired intellect.'[101]

Agent or Active Intellect Badawī has rightly characterized this intellect as the most important of this subset of four intellects.[102] Al-Fārābī tells us that

> when one has reached the acquired intellect, one will have reached that which is like the stars and one will have reached the limit to which those things which are related to hyle and matter ascend. When one ascends from this, then one will have ascended to the first stage of existing things which are immaterial, and the first stage is the stage of the agent intellect. The agent intellect which Aristotle mentioned in the third treatise of the *De Anima* is a separated form which never existed in matter nor ever will exist in it, and it is in a certain manner an intellect in actuality close in likeness to the acquired intellect. And the agent intellect is that principle which makes that essence which was an intellect in potentiality, an intellect in actuality and which makes the intelligibles which are intelligibles in potentiality, intelligibles in actuality.[103]

This Agent or Active Intellect is also identical to the Tenth Intellect which occupies a key role in the tenfold emanationist intellectual hierarchy of al-Fārābī, which has been described in more detail elsewhere,[104] but which will be alluded to again later in this chapter.

If this fourfold division of the fifth of the Fārābian Intellects *appears* to be the most complex and abstruse aspect of what we have surveyed thus far in al-Fārābī's theory of intellection, this is precisely because it *is*! So far I have let al-Fārābī, and some of his modern commentators like Fakhry and Badawī, state, reiterate and interpret the contents of the *Epistle on the Intellect* with regard to this particular fourfold division of the Fifth Intellect. It must be obvious, however, from reading quotations from this text, that some further clarification is needed. What is al-Fārābī really talking about?

Basically, in his sixfold list, al-Fārābī posits a fifth major species of intellection which has four different, but related and developing meanings, aspects or qualities. The relationship between each of these intellects is expressed in terms of matter and form, potentiality and actuality.[105] This fifth type of intellection has two opposite poles, passive and active, receptor and cause, which are respectively the Potential Intellect and the Active Intellect.[106] Between the two operate the Actual Intellect and the Acquired Intellect.[107] We may thus define, even if somewhat simplistically, as follows: Potential Intellect is that which has the *capacity* mentally to abstract and know the essence of things. It is a passive or latent quality.[108] Actual Intellect is that capacity *in action*.[109] Acquired Intellect is the latter in an externally *developing and developed* mode, the external factor being the *agency* of the Active Intellect.[110] The Active Intellect is the motor for this, the 'efficient cause' of thought, and also a cosmic link between the sublunary and transcendent worlds.[111] As Walzer puts it:

> The active intellect, *nous poiētikós*, is no longer identical with the divine mind ... but is described ... as a transcendent immaterial entity placed next to the sphere of the moon and acting as intermediary between the divine Mind and the human intellect in transmitting the divine emanation to the human soul once it has reached the stage of the acquired intellect.[112]

The key aspects of this whole fourfold multifaceted type of intellection reside in such significant English words as 'capacity', 'activation', 'development' and 'agency', which neatly encapsulate the Arabic data. We are talking, in other words, if we work from cause or motor to primary receptor, of a species of intellection being caused (through the *agency* of the Active Intellect) to *develop* as it *activates* its passive *capacity*. And the Matter–Form or Potentiality–Actuality relationship in this fourfold species of intellection is spelled out clearly by al-Fārābī in his text, as we have already seen: 'That essence which Aristotle in the *De Anima* calls intellect in potentiality … becomes intellect in actuality'; 'the intellect in actuality becomes now the acquired intellect'; 'the agent intellect … is in a certain manner an intellect in actuality close in likeness to the acquired intellect'.[113] The overlap and mutual interlocking of these varieties of the fifth major Fārābian type of intellection could not be clearer.

Sixth and last in this sixfold division of Fārābian intellects comes the First Principle, or Divine Reason – in other words, God Himself, who is the source of all intellection.[114] Al-Fārābī describes this supreme fount of all knowledge as follows in his famous *Epistle on the Intellect*:

> And it is not possible that the mover of the first heavens is the first principle for all existing things, but it has another principle necessarily. *This principle does not have a principle whose existence is more perfect than it. Since the mover of the first heavens is not matter nor in matter, it follows that it is an intellect in its substance and it thinks itself [or: its essence]* and the essence of that which is the principle of its existence. And it is clear that that which it thinks of the principle of its existence is more perfect than its two natures which are peculiar to it as the less perfect of them. Since its essence is divided into two natures it does not require anything besides these two. But that principle which is the principle through which the first heaven becomes a substance is necessarily one in all respects, and it is not possible that there is an existing thing more perfect than it, or that it have a principle. *Thus it is the principle of all principles and the first principle of all existing things.* And this is the intellect which Aristotle mentioned in letter Lam [book Lambda] of the *Metaphysics*. Each one of these others is also an intellect, but this one is the first intellect [*al-ʿAql al-Awwal*] and the first existing, the first one, and the first true. The others only become an intellect from it according to order.[115]

And with these words, after two further final, brief comments, al-Fārābī brings to a close his highly complex *Epistle on the Intellect* which has achieved a logical culmination in the source of all intellection, God Himself.

The above *sixfold* division of intellection is the first major aspect of

Fārābian theory. We may categorize it as the *Aristotelian* mode, register or dimension because of the way in which it is deliberately underpinned and supported by al-Fārābī himself with references to the works of Aristotle, for example the *De Anima* and the *Metaphysics*. This may all seem complicated enough. But there is more! Our Islamic philosopher has a second, parallel, *tenfold* scheme of intellection which this time clearly owes much to Neoplatonism, and may therefore be described as al-Fārābī's *Neoplatonic* mode, register or dimension of epistemology. I have elaborated this scheme in some depth elsewhere;[116] it may briefly be summarized as follows (Figure 2 provides an illustration of the interaction of the two registers): From God, The First, *emanates* a series of ten intellects, culminating in the Tenth Intellect which is the Agent or Active Intellect (*al-ʿAql al-Faʿʿāl*). The latter 'acts as a bridge between the heavenly or celestial world and the sublunary world. It thus has a highly specialized and distinctive role in al-Fārābī's cosmology.'[117] These intellects are associated with the production of the fixed stars, Saturn, Jupiter, Mars, the Sun, Venus, Mercury and the Moon.[118] A complicating and confusing feature to note, when comparing the Fārābian sixfold scheme of intellection with the tenfold, is that whereas in the sixfold scheme, the term 'First Intellect' (*al ʿAql al-Awwal*) is used at one point *of* God,[119] the First emanated Intellect is considered to be hypostatically '*distinct*' from God in the philosopher's tenfold scheme.

In summary, Fārābian epistemology must be considered to be an unsurprising mixture of the Aristotelian and the Neoplatonic. As Badawī puts it: 'Dans la théorie de la connaissance, al-Fârâbî fait une synthèse entre l'aristotélisme et le plotinisme, c'est-à-dire qu'il professe un empirisme complété par un mysticisme intuitioniste.'[120] Al-Fārābī has a two-dimensional theory of intellection, considerably broader in ambition and scope than many such theories produced and espoused today: astonishingly, it embraces the spheres of human cognition, sublunary agency and divine reason Itself.[121] The two epistemological registers are distinct but none the less touch and overlap at certain key points. Our conclusion must be that Fārābian thought provides a prototype epistemological paradigm of which the key aspect is the deliberate eclectic mix or counterpoint of the Aristotelian and the Neoplatonic. Readers may judge from the rest of this book whether other members of the 'School of Fārābī' articulated

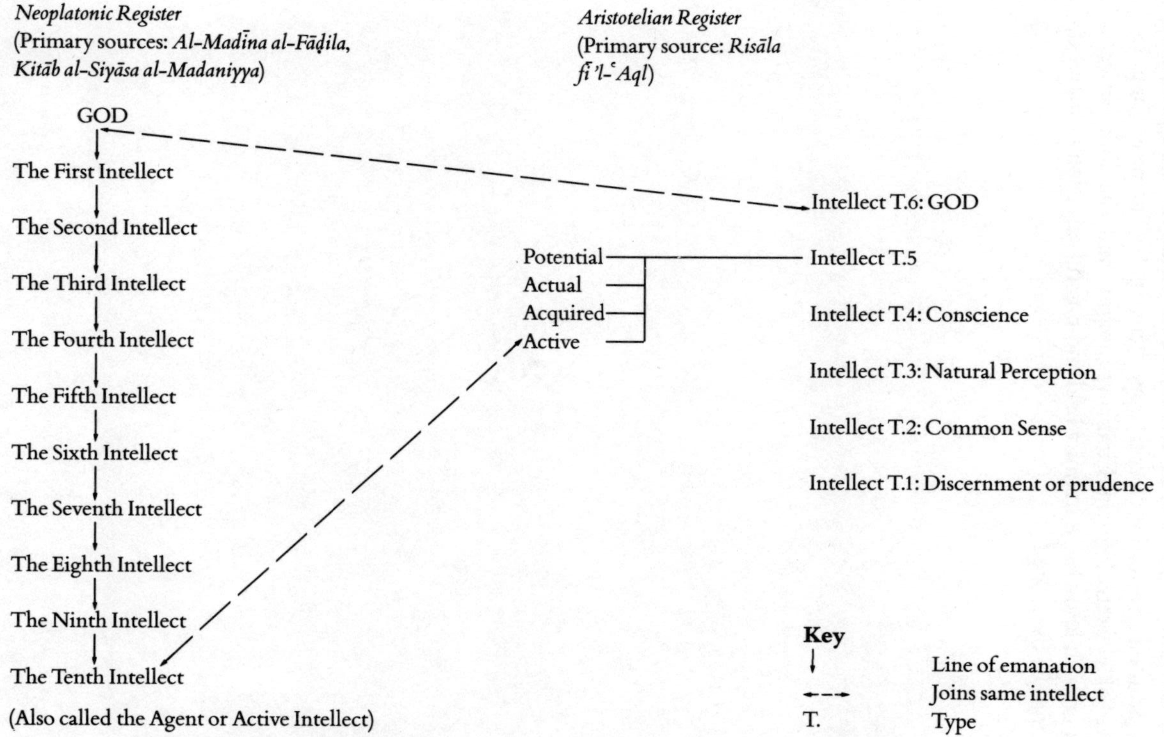
Neoplatonic Register
(Primary sources: Al-Madīna al-Fāḍila, Kitāb al-Siyāsa al-Madaniyya)
GOD
The First Intellect
The Second Intellect
The Third Intellect
The Fourth Intellect
The Fifth Intellect
The Sixth Intellect
The Seventh Intellect
The Eighth Intellect
The Ninth Intellect
The Tenth Intellect
(Also called the Agent or Active Intellect)
Aristotelian Register
(Primary source: Risāla fī'l-ʿAql)
Potential
Actual
Acquired
Active
Intellect T.6: GOD
Intellect T.5
Intellect T.4: Conscience
Intellect T.3: Natural Perception
Intellect T.2: Common Sense
Intellect T.1: Discernment or prudence
Key
Line of emanation
Joins same intellect
T.
Type

Figure 2 Al-Fārābī's epistemology: a basic archaeology

their epistemology in the same manner. Finally, it should be stressed here that Fārābian epistemology has a vital soteriological dimension as well: Majid Fakhry encapsulates this neatly when he observes: 'Like Aristotle, [al-Fārābī] assigns immortality to the intellectual part of the Soul only, or, to put it more accurately, he makes it contingent upon the Soul's degree of intellectual apprehension.'[122] The prime importance of epistemology in Fārābian thought, and the link between progress in knowledge in this world and blissful salvation in the next, cannot be overstated.

3

THE EPISTEMOLOGICAL SUBSTRATE OF FĀRĀBISM (ii): IN THE STEPS OF THEIR MASTER

The Elements of Yaḥyā b. ʿAdī's Epistemology

In the first chapter, during the brief survey of the life of Yaḥyā b. ʿAdī, we referred to two works by that author. They were his *Exposition of the Error of Abū Yūsuf Yaʿqūb ibn Isḥāq al-Kindī in his Treatise 'A Rebuttal of the Christians'* and the famous *Refinement of Character.* It is from these, together with two other works, that it is proposed to draw out in this chapter some of the major elements and facets of the epistemology of Yaḥyā b. ʿAdī. The two further works to which reference will be made are his short treatise entitled *On the Four Scientific Questions Regarding the Art of Logic (Maqāla fī 'l-Buḥūth al-Arbaʿa al-ʿIlmiyya ʿan Ṣināʿat al-Manṭiq)*,[1] and finally, the rather longer *Treatise on Divine Unity (Maqāla fī 'l-Tawḥīd)*.

Logic, both as an epistemological tool and a necessary prelude to the study of theology, occupied a favoured role in the development of Middle Eastern thought.[2]

> It is clear … that regardless of changes in approach and method, Muslim logicians never lost sight of the fact that the primary function of their labors was to find out about 'knowledge' and to contribute to a comprehensive epistemology for all aspects of Muslim intellectual endeavour, including theology and jurisprudence.[3]

In his introductory *Risāla* on logic, Yaḥyā's master, al-Fārābī, observed:

> Our purpose is the investigation of the art of logic, the art which includes the things which lead the rational faculty towards right thinking, wherever there is the possibility of error, and which indicates all the safeguards against error,

wherever a conclusion is to be drawn by the intellect (*al-ʿaql*). Its status in relation to the intellect (*al-ʿaql*) is the status of the art of grammar in relation to language, and just as the science of grammar rectifies the language among the people for whose language the grammar has been made, so the science of logic rectifies the intellect (*al-ʿaql*), so that it intellects only what is right where there is the possibility of error. Thus the relation of the science of grammar to the language and the expressions is as the relation of the science of logic to the intellect (*al-ʿaql*) and the intelligibles, and just as grammar is the touchstone of language where there is the possibility of an error of language in regard to the method of expression, so the science of logic is the touchstone of the intellect (*al-ʿaql*) where there is the possibility of an error in regard to the intelligibles.... The art of logic is an instrument by which, when it is employed in the several parts of philosophy, certain knowledge (*al-ʿilm al-yaqīn*) is obtained of all which the several theoretical and practical arts include, *and there is no way to certainty of the truth in anything of which knowledge is sought save the art of logic*.[4]

It is clear from this that, for al-Fārābī, logic acts as a kind of substrate, or deep structure *à la* Chomsky, for all else, including, of course, epistemology whose primary tool it is. Like master like pupil: it did not matter that the one was Muslim and the other Christian. It is clear that in both traditions logic achieved a primacy and veneration which was accorded to few other disciplines. It is interesting, too, that for both al-Fārābī and Yaḥyā, knowledge has a soteriological dimension. We examined al-Fārābī's own concept of this at the conclusion to chapter 2. Here we might note the words with which Yaḥyā commences his treatise *On the Four Scientific Questions regarding the Art of Logic.* He states that these questions are 'whether it is, what it is, which thing it is, and why it is. He entitles it: *Guidance for Those who are Lost to the Path of Salvation*[5] (*al-Hidāya li-man Tāha ilā Sabīl al-Najāt*).[6] One may, perhaps, extrapolate from all this and not exaggerate too wildly if one states that for both al-Fārābī and Yaḥyā b. ʿAdī, logic constituted one of the vital keys to salvation and so, to Paradise itself.[7]

In this treatise, Yaḥyā then continues by examining firstly the usefulness of logic. He laments that the ignorance or quarrelsome nature of many people made such a demonstration necessary, and maintains that 'the benefit deriving from the art of logic is intrinsic not accidental, and this can be seen in its definition. It is *an instrumental art by which one discriminates between truth and falsehood in theoretical science, and between good and evil in practical science*.'[8] The good acquired by logic is 'complete happiness'.[9] In a passage important for the understanding of his epistemology, Yaḥyā goes on to state that knowledge may be acquired in one of two principal ways: (1) either *without* the use of logic and reference to prior knowledge by means of such faculties as imagination, perception and what Yaḥyā terms the '*first principles of reason* which cannot be proved' or (2) *with* the use of logic by means of 'inference, syllogism and proof', involving a reference to prior knowledge.[10]

Yaḥyā then goes on to make a substantial 'Digression on the Sources of Error'. He emphasizes that such faculties as 'reason, perception and thought' only work properly and convey real and true knowledge if they are 'in a state of health and freedom from the corrupting infirmities which make it fail in its purpose'. But distortion may result if the senses or imaginative faculty are in any way impaired. In a statement which would certainly have fuelled Plato's general scepticism about data garnered via the senses and which, with its references to black and yellow bile, peddles the usual humoral theory of the Middle Ages, Yaḥyā concludes that it is possible 'to taste the sweet bitter, the bitter sweet'. And mental incapacity parallels faulty sensory perception: 'The same thing happens to reason if the instrument with which it does its work, the brain, is sick. Then its conceiving and what it conceives are corrupted.'[11] The syllogism itself, Yaḥyā observes, depending on how it is framed, can yield false conclusions.[12]

We may revert for a moment to our two basic epistemological questions of *what* can be known and *how* it can be known, and examine these two with reference to the brief treatise which we have just surveyed. Clearly, the treatise deals much with the *modes* of acquiring knowledge, with its references to perception, imagination, syllogism, inference and proof. But it also clearly underlines the fact that *what* we can know may rest on shifting sands: the 'knowledge' garnered by the hallucinating wanderer in the desert of an oasis of palm trees and running springs clearly conflicts with reality! There is, in other words, in Yaḥyā's epistemology a real Platonic appreciation of the nature of what may be known. And it is not only the senses which may yield false results but the path of logic itself. Perception and logic both share an intrinsic fallibility, and that, to revert to what was stated earlier, may have serious consequences for salvation itself.

Logic may indeed yield happiness in this life but false logic may yield eternal unhappiness in the next.

We turn now to an examination of the second of the four works proposed above for analysis, *The Refinement of Character.* It is proposed here to accept that the argument over the actual authorship of this work is exhausted, indeed dead, and that the work is truly the product of Yaḥyā b. ʿAdī.[13] If we hold that the short treatise *On the Four Scientific Questions Regarding the Art of Logic* stresses the primacy of logic, and its epistemological link to *personal salvation*, then the longer *Refinement of Character* emphasizes the link between ethics, politics and knowledge.

There is no doubt that *The Refinement of Character* lacks originality,[14] but its early position in the history of Islamic ethics makes it particularly significant and interesting.[15] Walzer summarized its principal features thus:

> The treatise *Fī Tahdhīb al-Akhlāḳ* of the Jacobite philosopher Yaḥyā b. ʿAdī represents another variant of late Greek thought. There are no specifically Christian ideas in it; Aristotelian influence is, as in al-Rāzī, non-existent. It is based on the Platonic tripartition of the soul, but the 21 virtues and corresponding vices are neither specifically referred to the three souls nor subordinated to the four cardinal virtues and their contraries (which are listed among them). This scheme probably depends ultimately on some lost pre-neoplatonic Greek original. His concluding chapter on the perfect man who bases his life *on the requirements of his intellectual soul* and has trained himself to love every human being combines stoic and neoplatonic language, and is not very different from the thought of al-Fārābī.[16]

In his edition of *The Refinement of Character*, al-Takriti draws our attention to Yaḥyā's usage of such phrases as 'cogitation and discrimination' (*fikr wa tamyīz*) instead of the expected word for 'intellect' and 'reason' (*ʿaql*), and to the fact that Yaḥyā also eschews an exact definition of the concept of reason.[17] However, despite this lack of formal definition at the beginning of *The Refinement of Character*, and slightly differing nomenclature employed, it is perfectly clear what Yaḥyā is talking about and there is no reason why, for the sake of economy, *fikr wa tamyīz* should not be rendered simply, even if loosely, as 'reason'. This 'reason' is the primary criterion which distinguishes man from other forms of life.[18] And the use of reason for man is a very real necessity, not an optional luxury: if man abandons himself to the innately evil qualities in his nature and ignores his reason, he is a self-chosen victim of pure animal morality (*akhlāq al-bahā'im*) because it is precisely his reason which should set him apart from the animals.[19] Because of man's natural disposition towards evil there is a profound need for the proper rule of law and right-living kings.[20]

One may be forgiven for wondering whether Yaḥyā's pessimism about human nature does not reflect in some way the Christian theologians' doctrine of original sin. Whatever the case, however, it is clear that here, for Yaḥyā, ethics and politics are ineluctably linked.[21] Yaḥyā clearly wishes to stress that the *internal* structure of a man's thoughts, moral dispositions and passions can, at the very least, have serious *outward political* consequences. Morally good men clearly have the capacity to become morally good kings and rulers. Kings who live rightly and laws that are good will, in Yaḥyā's own words, 'prevent the evildoer from his iniquity, obstruct the usurper from his usurpation and punish the libertine for his debauchery'.[22] The implied corollary of all this is that, given a bad king and bad laws, the evil desires of all men's hearts – those of ruler and ruled alike – will dominate and flourish. Chaos rather than good order will ensue.

What is needed is some form of *control*, not in the shape of an intellect trained by unthinking, fascist Orwellian thought-police, but in the guise of a well-endowed intellect equipped with real knowledge. Here now appears a stress on reason, i.e. on what might be termed the third main element here of Yaḥyā b. ʿAdī's epistemological circle: this is the circle which links – or should link – together in a coherent harmony *ethics*, *politics* and *reason* or *knowledge*. If the three points on the circumference are joined – and provided, of course, that we intend by these terms properly formed ethics, producing just politics based upon well-ordered and sound reason and knowledge, which is, once again, in turn the foundation of good conscience and properly formed ethics – then the radii of the circle point inwards towards a central point of ultimate personal perfection and human happiness for ruled and ruler[23] (see Figure 3). And it is self-evident that such perfection must provide an infallible key to salvation in Paradise. Yaḥyā, as a Christian, would have much appreciated the New Testament injunction: 'You are to be perfect, as your heavenly Father is perfect.'[24] Further, as we saw before, the 'happiness' aspect has a related epistemological dimension: the good acquired by logic is 'complete happiness',[25] and it was suggested that it might not be fanciful to assume that, for Yaḥyā, logic itself might constitute a vital passport to salvation.

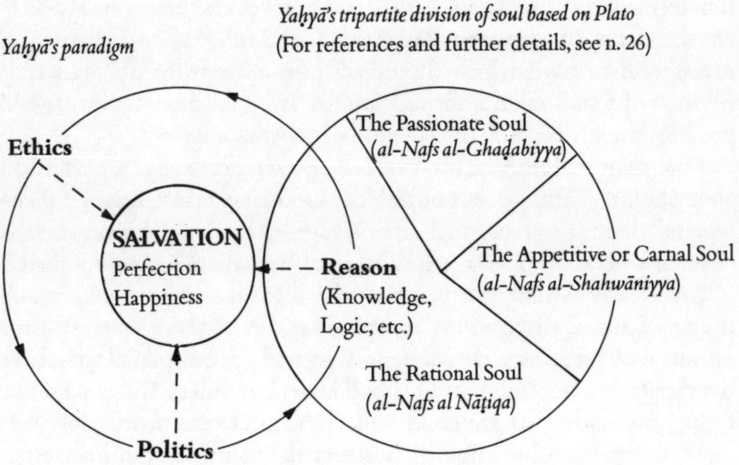

Figure 3 The moral and soteriological epistemology of Yaḥyā b. ʿAdī

Yaḥyā's *Control* is that major faculty of Plato's division of soul (see Figure 3) which Yaḥyā calls 'The Rational Soul' (*al-Nafs al-Nāṭiqa*).[26] By it, man is distinguished from all the animals, for it comprises a package of key features which no animal possesses, namely, cogitation, thinking (*al-fikr*), memory (*al-dhikr*), discrimination, discernment (*al-tamyīz*) and comprehension (*al-fahm*).[27] The passage where these details occur is a good example of Yaḥyā's preferred choice of words like *fikr* and *tamyīz* instead of — but as synonyms for — *ʿaql* (intellect, reason).[28] Al-Takriti concludes: 'We notice that he used the terms reason, rational soul, thinking and discernment in the meaning of man's self-control, that is man is able to do good, follow virtue and avoid vice and bad actions.'[29] Ethical choice clearly has an epistemological quality, for it is based on knowledge.[30] Man can fortify and strengthen his rational soul by the study of 'the rational sciences' (*al-ʿulūm al-ʿaqliyya*), and the study of books dealing with ethics and politics.[31] Here again is the stress on Yaḥyā's primary link of ethics, politics and reason.

It has been well pointed out that 'Yaḥyā's ideas on ethical behaviour, the three souls and the just man, are similar to those of Plato in his *Republic*.'[32] Al-Takriti has also demonstrated convincingly the impact of Aristotle's *Nicomachean Ethics* on Yaḥyā's *Refinement of Character*[33] and, in the light of al-Takriti's careful analysis, Walzer's comment that 'Aristotelian influence is, as in al-Rāzī, non-existent'[34] rings somewhat strangely. Al-Takriti notes, furthermore, 'some agreement with Galen and Plotinus'[35] and this does concur with Walzer's remarks that Yaḥyā's 'concluding chapter on the perfect man ... combines stoic and neoplatonic language, and is not very different from the thought of al-Fārābī'.[36] However, the role of Neoplatonism is fairly minimal in this text by comparison with that of Platonism. What we have here is a text that follows a *Platonic-Aristotelian* paradigm rather than the *Aristotelian–Neoplatonic* one adumbrated above. Walzer is right, however, to hint at the impact of al-Fārābī on Yaḥyā and this point is developed in greater detail by al-Takriti who notes: 'Al-Farabi always considered Ethics as the most important influence on a man's life. As logic provides the rules and regulations in knowledge, so Ethics yields the fundamental rules and laws which should be followed by man in his dealings with his fellow men.'[37] He points out that al-Fārābī too believed that virtue was the product of education and knowledge.[38] It is clear, then, from this that Yaḥyā follows a basically Fārābian model in his linking of the ethical and the intellectual.

The remaining two texts by Yaḥyā, which we cited earlier, may be dealt with more briefly. In his *Exposition of the Error*,[39] which is a defence of the Christian dogma of the Trinity in response to a critique by al-Kindī, Yaḥyā couches his reply in the same Aristotelian and Porphyrian vocabulary as his opponent. Fakhry has emphasized that some of 'his analogies are significantly drawn from emanationism',[40] though later the same commentator stresses, having discussed some other texts by Yaḥyā, that 'on the question of creation, Yaḥia, unlike his Muslim Neo-Platonic master, al-Fārābī, stands unequivocally behind the protagonists of creation *ex nihilo*'.[41] What we have, however, in the *Exposition* is a discussion in terms of al-Kindī's Aristotelianism, the five 'voices' or 'predicables' of the Neoplatonist Porphyry of Tyre (AD 234–*c.* 305) (one of Plotinus' disciples and his editor), together with the faint shadow of emanation hanging over the text, thus bringing the whole close to the Aristotelian-Neoplatonic paradigm by which many another work from the 'School of Fārābī' is characterized. And if we ask of this text, '*What* can be known?', Yaḥyā's theological response will be, 'The Trinity'. The modality of that knowledge clearly comes not simply, or even mainly, via the eye of faith but through the Aristotelian–Neoplatonic sieve to which we have referred. It is clear that, for Yaḥyā, the Trinity can be explained and defended according to the norms of dialectical philosophy, even if (though he does not say this) it cannot be fully understood. In this treatise, at least, Yaḥyā does not communicate any sense of the *mystery* of his subject; he is content to stress the use of *reason* and reasoned argument.

The *Treatise on Divine Unity*[42] is also much influenced by Aristotle, in particular by that author's *Metaphysics*, but also – unexpectedly – by Procline doctrine as well, directly or indirectly.[43] This treatise first surveys a variety of views concerning God's unity before Yaḥyā provides his own, concluding 'that the First Cause has plurality only in virtue of the constituent parts of its definition, viz. the attributes which may be predicated of the divine essence'.[44] Yaḥyā believes that 'these attributes, which are three, can be deduced from His creation – His substance is hidden, but His essence is evident from His activity: bounty (*jūd* = *agathótēs*), power (*qudra* = *dúnamis*) and wisdom (*ḥikma* = *gnōsis*)'.[45] Endress stresses the Procline nature of this triad,[46] as does Yaḥyā's editor, Khalil Samir.[47] The latter maintains that the *Treatise on Divine Unity* is entirely based on the work of Aristotle and his commentators.[48] The Procline triad towards the end, however, is significant and means that this work too, like *The Exposition of the Error* surveyed above, has what may at least be described as a 'Neoplatonic flavour', even though there is no question of emanation in Yaḥyā's work here. The combination of Aristotle and the Neoplatonist Proclus Diadochus (AD 410–85) in this Christian text is an intriguing one, and both Endress and Samir hint at Pseudo-Dionysius as a possible vehicle for the Procline doctrine. Endress notes:

> In the philosophy of Proclus, 'Goodness, Power and Knowledge constitute the primary divine triad … which prefigures in a seminal form the triad of the second hypostasis, Being, Life and Intelligence …'. The Procline doctrine reappears in Ps.-Dionysius Areopagita, *whose influence on Yaḥyā ibn ʿAdī deserves further investigation.*[49]

The editor of Yaḥyā's *Treatise on Divine Unity*, Khalil Samir, appears to concur:[50] and both Endress and Samir are agreed that the ultimate source of the triad lies in Proclus' *Elements of Theology*.[51] Later, of course, Yaḥyā would replace this triad of *jūd*, *qudra* and *ḥikma* with a much more famous one, by which he would designate God: *ʿaql*, *ʿāqil*, *maʿqūl*.[52] I have rendered this phrase loosely elsewhere as 'pure, thinking, intelligible mind',[53] but it must be noted that Yaḥyā's terminology of the intellect has a Christian Trinitarian dimension as well:

In consistency with Alfarabi's philosophy of religion, according to which religious motifs are symbols of philosophical truths, Ibn ʿAdī treated theological notions as embodiments of philosophical concepts. For example, he interprets the persons of the Trinity as symbolic representations of Aristotelian ideas: the Father symbolizes the intellect; the Son symbolizes the intellectually cognizing subject, and the Spirit symbolizes the intellectually cognized object.[54]

We may conclude briefly, from our study of these four works by Yaḥyā b. ʿAdī, that the author is much more dependent on Plato and Aristotle for his epistemology than he is on Aristotle plus Plotinus, though we should not, I suppose, lose sight of Proclus. However, Yaḥyā's concept of intellect, for example, owes nothing to the tenfold emanationist hierarchy of his master, al-Fārābī. The disciple has felt free to float away from his teacher and there is thus no question of duplicating the basic Fārābian Aristotelian-Neoplatonic paradigm adumbrated in chapter 2, except in the faintest way. (If anything, Yaḥyā exhibits much more of what we have called a Platonic-Aristotelian paradigm.) Where, however, Yaḥyā is a true pupil is in his reiteration of another Fārābian theme: for the Second Master too, established a link between ethics, politics and reason.[55]

Al-Sijistānī and Knowledge

We referred earlier, in chapter 1, to the major work of al-Sijistānī entitled *The Cupboard of Wisdom.* The importance of this work should not be underestimated. Fakhry has noted:

> Nicknamed the logician, al-Sijistānī is said to have written numerous commentaries on Aristotelian logic and related subjects, but unfortunately none of these works has come down to us. In fact, with the exception of al-Tauḥīdī's account of his philosophical and logical views, we have no other clue to his thought except the cursory, if complimentary, references to him by the later historians of philosophy.[56]

Josef Van Ess confirms that we know al-Sijistānī 'mostly through scattered remarks which were noted down by his companion Abū Ḥayyān al-Tawḥīdī'.[57] None the less, his remarks are clearly not intended to belittle *The Cupboard of Wisdom* which, indeed, as Kraemer reminds us, 'is our only source for as-Sijistânî's early period'.[58] It may not have been absolutely original, but its comprehensive nature was recognized and applauded from medieval times.[59] And al-Sijistānī's vast Greek learning, upon which Fakhry has commented,[60] is evident from the briefest glance at the names of the Greek and Islamic philosophers and writers whose histories in one form or another are contained within the Arabic text of *The Cupboard*. They include well-known figures like Thales of Miletus, Pythagoras, Socrates, Plato, Aristotle, Homer, Euclid, Hippocrates, Ptolemy, Euripides, Thucydides, Sophocles, Plotinus, Philo, Porphyry and Galen on the one hand; and Yaḥyā al-Naḥwī (John Philoponus), Ḥunayn b. Isḥāq, al-Kindī, al-ʿĀmirī and Yaḥyā b. ʿAdī, on the other.[61] (The latter two, of course, are covered in some depth in this book.)

The Cupboard of Wisdom, then, shows al-Sijistānī functioning as a major *historian* of philosophy. But if we wish to examine him as a philosopher *in his own right*, and try and glean some ideas about his theories of intellection and general epistemology, we are better served by referring to the work of al-Tawḥīdī, as suggested and noted above by Fakhry and Van Ess. We might usefully, therefore, using such sources, survey first al-Sijistānī's views about the soul and the intellect.

At times, it is clear that al-Sijistānī thinks in terms of a *Platonic* tripartite division of the soul like Yaḥyā b. ʿAdī: for example, al-Sijistānī 'associated with the Platonic doctrine of the tripartition of the soul corresponding virtues. He quoted Plato: "Whoever rules his reason is called wise; whoever rules his anger is called courageous; and whoever rules his passion is called temperate."'[62] But al-Sijistānī is also familiar with an *Aristotelian* tripartite division of soul into the vegetative (*al-nāmiyya*), animal (*al-ḥayawāniyya*) and rational (*al-nāṭiqa*).[63] What is interesting and relevant about both of these divisions, the Platonic and the Aristotelian, is that they both clearly possess a clear and important *rational* element.

In another place al-Sijistānī defines the soul as 'a divine force which mediates between Nature (*al-Ṭabīʿa*) … and the Intellect (*al-ʿAql*)'. Just as man has a nature whose effects are apparent in his body, so too is he blessed with an intelligence which enables him to discriminate and undertake a whole range of other intellectual functions.[64]

However, despite this range of divisions, influences and definitions, al-Sijistānī is forced to admit that it is really very difficult to describe the soul adequately.[65] Aristotle, as Kraemer points out, confessed to a similar problem at the beginning of his *De Anima*.[66] Al-

Sijistānī more than hints that the reason for this lies in a third dimension of the soul, over and above the Platonic and Aristotelian; that dimension is the Neoplatonic. Al-Sijistānī 'observes that it is difficult for man to know the soul, for he can only know the soul by means of his soul, and he is veiled from his soul by his soul. For he is compound, his soul simple. Also, he contains a small part of soul, and a part of soul can hardly know its totality.'[67] Here we have a clear reference to the classical Neoplatonic doctrine of the Universal Soul, of which man's soul is but a part;[68] and it has been stressed that it is the *Neoplatonic* dimension in al-Sijistānī's various discussions about the soul which is the one which prevails.[69]

For this brief survey, it is clear that al-Sijistānī, at various points in his writings, considers the question of soul under the three distinct headings of the Platonic, the Aristotelian and the Neoplatonic. Each, it will be observed, has a noetic quality: the Platonic and the Aristotelian both posit a rational soul; the Neoplatonic stresses more the *unknowability* of soul and this, of course, reflects the general Neoplatonic attitude towards the One, the Deity Himself, who is supremely 'Unknowable'. Kraemer comments:

> The notion that the human soul is a small part of the universal soul – the doctrine of monopsychism – is affiliated with the idea that man is a microcosmic replica of the cosmic hierarchy in the sense that he is endowed with nature, soul and intellect. He does not contain the One in the same way but has cognition of it. It is implied that the One is glimpsed by means of contemplation of the great chain of being.[70]

The above remarks are designed to be a short introduction to what will now follow, that is, a survey of al-Sijistānī's doctrine of intellection and his general epistemology. Once again it is necessary to go to al-Tawḥīdī for most of our references. The question may be posed: does al-Sijistānī in his treatment of the intellect, embrace Platonic, Aristotelian and Neoplatonic definitions and does the latter dominate as it does in the case of the soul?

Al-Sijistānī's theory of intellection has something in common with al-Fārābī's sixfold division of the intellect (reflecting as it does aspects of the fifth Fārābian intellect), as well as that same philosopher's emanationist hierarchy of ten intellects, where the Tenth Intellect is also called the Agent or Active Intellect. However, it is worth stressing that in what follows, the text upon which these remarks are based, here at least, 'represents an attempt to arrive at a proper definition of terms; it is not a systematic exposition of the process of intellection'.[71]

In what has been identified as 'our principal source for as-Sijistâ-nî's doctrine of intellect',[72] Abū Ḥayyān al-Tawḥīdī's *The Conversations (al-Muqābasāt)*, al-Sijistānī identifies three types of intellect. There is the Agent or Active Intellect (*al-ʿAql al-Faʿʿāl*) which is paralleled in both the Fārābian schemes or divisions alluded to above; there is the Human Intellect (*al-ʿAql al-Insānī*) which is also known as the Material Intellect (*al-ʿAql al-Hayūlānī*); and, finally, there is the Acquired Intellect (*al-ʿAql al-Mustafād*) which parallels an aspect of al-Fārābī's Fifth Intellect, in his sixfold division. These three intellects of al-Sijistānī – Active, Human and Acquired – are viewed in terms of agent, patient and action (*fāʿil, mafʿūl, fiʿl*) respectively.[73] Kraemer believes that the text of the *Muqābasāt* here implicitly assumes an identification between the Aristotelian or Neo-Aristotelian Active Intellect and the Neoplatonic Intellect, and also points to the key doctrine in Neoplatonism of the unity of the intellect.[74] Elsewhere, al-Sijistānī stresses that the intellect is the vital link between the corporeal and incorporeal worlds.[75] People may indeed differ in the types of intellect which they possess,[76] but ultimately all are a part of the same majestic hypostasis. Badawī believes that al-Sijistānī attributes to the intellect qualitites comparable to those which Plotinus accords to the *Nous.*[77] He believes that al-Sijistānī endows reason with a divine force and quotes, in support, the following view of his via al-Tawḥīdī's *Book of Pleasure and Conviviality*: 'The intellect (*al-ʿaql*) is the Caliph of God. It is the recipient of the pure emanation (*al-fayḍ al-khāliṣ*) which has neither blemish nor impurity. If one said that intellect were absolute light (lit. *nūr fī 'l-ghāya*) one would not be far wrong.'[78]

This reference to emanation highlights once again the Neoplatonic dimension of al-Sijistānī's thought; and before moving from this brief survey of the components of his theory of intellection to his general epistemological views, it is worth spending a little longer stressing the Neoplatonic context of all his thinking. For his Neoplatonism is not an optional or peripheral extra but an integral part of what he believed and taught. This, of course, has profound implications for any theory of intellection given the dominant role played by the Universal Intellect and its clones and hypostatic subordinates in classical Islamic Neoplatonism.

Of al-Sijistāni, S.M. Stern wrote: 'His system, like that of most of the other members of his environment, had a strong Neo-platonic colouring.'[79] We have already noted above the reference by al-Sijistānī to emanation (*fayḍ*) and his analogy with light. Elsewhere, the intellect is compared to the sun; the soul is its deputy (*khalīfatuhu*) but the intellect is brighter than the soul and whereas the sun is subject to setting, rising and eclipse, the radiance of the intellect is eternal (*ishrāqahu dā'im*).[80]

In one of his short philosophical treatises, *On the Specific Perfection of the Human Species*, al-Sijistānī adds to our picture of the Neoplatonic dimension of the intellect.

> [It is] the cause of the order of existents and their harmonious combination, giving each of them its determined existence. Each of them seeks the help of intellect for its specific perfection.... Intellect has two other functions: the first, insofar as it is primary, simple, activated, and caused by the First Cause and First Agent, praised and exalted, which gives each existent – intellect, soul, and what is beneath them – the existence common to all of them. Intellect allots this existence to the essences of existents by giving them the forms specific to each one of them.... The second function is what [intellect] performs by means of soul by conferring life upon everything ready to receive it. This activity belongs to soul *per se* and to [intellect] by its intermediacy. For soul is the form that occurs in the animate being, and intellect bestows it. [Intellect], therefore, is what merits being called 'complete', 'universal', 'perfect', and 'perfecting others'. Or [intellect] has completeness by virtue of the First Agent, insofar as it made it cause of the existence of every existent by ordering existents in harmonious relations.[81]

Apart from the Neoplatonic activities described above, what is particularly fascinating about this short treatise, as implied by its title *On the Specific Perfection of the Human Species*, is that it was written specifically for the Būyid prince, whose patronage he gained, namely ʿAḍud al-Dawla. In Kraemer's words, 'he is the perfect individual whose manifestation is celebrated in this treatise'.[82] God's power (lit. 'the power emanated from the Ultimate Foundation') descends through the emanationist hierarchy or chain, a veritable purveyor of virtues, which are then embodied in this world in one of pure soul and intellect who is fitted thereby to rule the world of men, save them from tyrants and establish a just hierarchy. Al-Sijistānī clearly intends that this should parallel in a corporeal and temporal fashion, the ordered hierarchy of Neoplatonism in the celestial sphere where the intellect and the soul know their exact rank and are eternally obedient to the hypostasis above them; in a similar fashion mankind should order itself.[83] Here then, the Neoplatonic emphasis on, indeed fetish for, order and hierarchy provides the ethos for this whole treatise with the ordering of the supralunary world as an eternally emanated paradigm for all behaviour in the sublunary sphere. In other words, this Neoplatonism of al-Sijistānī has a political and ethical dimension or edge.

Having examined some of the key aspects of al-Sijistānī's theory of intellection, and noted its Neoplatonic orientation, we will move now to some other areas of that philosopher's general epistemology. He has much to say on the subject of knowledge; the following aphoristic statements help to set the scene: just as the *intellect* is compared to absolute light and to the sun (see above), so light imagery is employed when al-Sijistānī talks about *knowledge*. For example, after the citation of Plato's remark that 'Knowledge is the lamp of the soul', al-Sijistānī remarks: 'How beautiful is that lamp whose glass is pure, whose light is sharp, whose oil is strong and whose wick is straight.'[84] In *The Cupboard of Wisdom*, al-Sijistānī quotes Theognis' observation that 'Knowledge (*al-ʿIlm*) is not on the level of food which suffices to feed two or three but cannot feed many persons. Rather, it is like light (*ka 'l-nūr*) which enables many eyes to see all at the same time.'[85] Elsewhere al-Sijistānī holds that

> Knowledge (*al-ʿIlm*) and wealth are like two wives [of the same man]. They rarely go together and are reconciled to each other. Also, a man's portion of wealth results from the concupiscent and bestial soul (*al-Nafs al-Shahawiyya*) whereas his portion of knowledge results from the rational soul (*al-Nafs al-ʿĀqila*). These two portions oppose and contradict each other. Further, a discerning and discriminating person must realize that a man who possesses knowledge is nobler in every conceivable respect than a man of wealth. If he is given knowledge, he need not despair of money, of which a little suffices, or greatly worry about the loss of it. Knowledge exercises control. Wealth is something over which control is exercised. Knowledge belongs to the soul. Wealth is corporeal. Knowledge belongs to a man in a more personal manner than wealth. The perils of the wealthy are many and sudden. You do not see a man who possesses knowledge robbed of his knowledge and left deprived of it. But you have seen quite a few people whose money was stolen, taken away or confiscated, and the former owners remained helpless and destitute. *Knowledge thrives on being spent.* It accom-

panies its possessor into destitution. It makes it possible to be satisfied with little. It lowers a curtain over need. Wealth does not do that.[86]

This extended passage of al-Sijistānī's view on the relative merits of wealth and knowledge requires little commentary: it vaunts the values of knowledge and is highly Platonic both in its attitude to things corporeal and corporeal need, and its reference to the rational and concupiscent souls. A neat equation is drawn with things material and temporal like money (*al-māl*) deriving from the concupiscent, bestial or appetitive soul, while that which has an eternal quality and cannot, as al-Sijistānī points out, be taken away, is associated with the rational soul. Thus an ancient and perennial dichotomy between soul or mind on the one hand, and matter on the other, underlies this text purveying al-Sijistānī's ideas, which looks both backwards to Plato and forwards, in some respects, to Descartes. And here too, as with the intellect, there is an ethical dimension to the discussion.

All the above quotations show the premium that al-Sijistānī placed on knowledge (*ʿilm*): the latter is truly the fruit or the yield of the intellect (*al-ʿilm thamarat al-ʿAql*).[87] And while the truth born of knowledge may often be partial rather than total – and here he retells the famous Buddhist[88] parable of the elephant and the blind men, each of whom describes that animal differently according to the limb which he touches[89] – this can never invalidate the need to search for that truth which is the product, or partial product, of knowledge. For the truth brings men together, while error divides them.[90] It is interesting, of course, from the point of view of Plato's suspicion of the data yielded by sensory perception,[91] that the parable of the elephant is retold by al-Sijistānī after the latter has briefly quoted Plato himself. None the less, al-Sijistānī's epistemology is clearly not denying a validity or role to any knowledge gleaned by the senses but simply pointing out its limitations as indicated in this well-known parable. In this respect, al-Sijistānī cannot be described as an unreconstructed Platonist. The specific point made by his citation of the parable here, however, is that 'we find all those professing a doctrine to be determined by his own perspective, prejudice, nature and passion. But the far-ranging, intelligent and thorough person nevertheless has an advantage over others.'[92]

Jadaane neatly summarizes al-Sijistānī's epistemology thus: he maintains that it follows two distinct lines, one Greek, the other Graeco-Muslim. In consequence, two types or modes of knowledge can be identified: natural knowledge and supernatural knowledge. The quest for truth may certainly be difficult but it is possible. Thus agnosticism and scepticism are rejected.[93] Jadaane emphasizes[94] that knowledge in al-Sijistānī is defined as the image of the object known in the soul of the knowing subject (*al-ʿilm ṣūrat al-maʿlūm fī nafs al-ʿālim*).[95] The souls of the learned (*al-ʿulamāʾ*) are actually (*bi ʾl-fiʿl*) knowledgeable; the souls of the pupils (*al-mutaʿallimūn*) are potentially (*bi ʾl-quwwa*) knowledgeable.[96] After such vocabulary it is hardly surprising that Jadaane rightly chooses to conclude: the natural epistemology of al-Sijistānī is profoundly Aristotelian in its inspiration, while his 'supernatural' epistemology has its roots in the Greek mythological tradition on the one hand and Qur'ānic revelation on the other.[97]

Al-Sijistānī's general overall epistemology then, may be said to have elements of the Platonic and elements of the Aristotelian, while being neither totally Platonic nor totally Aristotelian. And there is a third element in his epistemological cauldron and that is the *Neoplatonic*. We have stressed already the Neoplatonic dimension of Sijistānian thought. It is also clearly apparent in the following epistemological division: in response to a question, al-Sijistānī notes that there are four grades of knowledge:

1. There is that which is purely sensible (*maḥsūs baḥt*), possessed, for example, by the animals;
2. there is that which is purely intellectual or intelligible (*maʿqūl maḥḍ*) and is characteristic of the celestial bodies;
3. there is that which is both sensible and intellectual (*maḥsūs maʿqūl*) which is associated with man's imagination; and
4. finally, there is that which is both intellectual and sensible (*maʿqūl maḥsūs*) which the perspicacious man (*dhū ʾl-naẓar*) attains by some piece of research (*bi ʾl-baḥth*).[98]

Al-Sisjistānī continues: the more a man thus studies and researches carefully, the greater his chance of attaining to 'the knowledge (*ʿilm*)[99] of the rational and living bodies, which are free from sensory perception (*al-ḥiss*) thanks to what they possess of the eternal emanation (*al-fayḍ al-dāʾim*)'.[100] Man's soul will then be illuminated with real knowledge; his conduct or way of life will be upright and on a rational course; and his character or morals will be purified of all material filth; this is clearly the highest form of human knowledge.[101] The mixture of Platonism (with its constant distaste for sensory perception) and Neoplatonism (with its reference to emanation) only highlights the eclecticism of Sijistānian thought. And, as Jadaane stresses, there is a neat equivalence between these four grades of knowledge and the fourfold hierarchy of animals, celestial bodies, ordinary men and pure, 'illuminated' men, into which latter category, of course, fall the philosopher, the astrologer, the soothsayer and the prophet.[102]

With the link now established above between real knowledge and morality, we may turn briefly and finally to a consideration of the ethics proper of al-Sijistānī, a subject upon which we have already touched several times. As will be abundantly clear from what has gone before, al-Sijistānī's philosophy is impregnated with a divine moral ethos.[103] Philosophy and morality do, indeed, go hand in hand. And we can say that, just as, for al-Sijistānī, knowledge is the fruit of the intellect,[104] so virtue, or the virtues (*al-faḍā'il*), are the fruit of a well-ordered desire associated with the intellect.[105]

Al-Sijistānī lists wisdom (*al-ḥikma*) as one of the sensory (or perceptible) and intellectual virtues (*al-faḍā'il al-ḥissiyya wa 'l-ʿaqliyya*) in a group which also includes courage, generosity, gentleness (or discernment) (*ḥilm*) and patience.[106] This characterization of the virtues as *ḥissiyya* and *ʿaqliyya* interestingly parallels those epithets of *maḥsūs* and *maʿqūl* in al-Sijistānī's fourfold gradation of knowledge which we studied earlier.[107] There is, then, an apparent harmony or parallelism of language as well as content, at least here in these two places, in the treatment of knowledge and virtue, which leads almost inexorably to the formulation of a basic paradigm in which we suggest that, for al-Sijistānī, in some senses at least, knowledge *is* virtue and virtue *is* knowledge.

In conclusion, then, it is clear that if knowledge is bound up with virtue and good ethics, then the latter in turn are bound up with salvation itself. And if the middle term of this proposition (ethics) is omitted, then we can say that salvation has a real epistemological quality or dimension in the thought of al-Sijistānī. But ethics are important and, as Kraemer stresses, 'not only the intellect but the moral virtues as well are related to the divine'.[108] Good ethics for al-Sijistānī, emphasizes al-Takriti, 'control' the soul[109] while good thinking keeps one on the right path and free of sense-inspired error.[110] Plato would certainly have agreed! However, it is 'a modified Platonic doctrine' which lies at the heart of Sijistānian ethics: 'Whereas in Platonic ethics, courage is related to the rationally-directed spiritual faculty, Abū Sulaymān al-Sijistānī relates it to all three faculties of the soul, thus giving rise to three kinds of courage.'[111] This is illustrated in the following quotation: 'If courage is rational, it facilitates the pursuit of wisdom, persistence in attaining the goal, and expending energy to obtain desire. If it is spiritual, it facilitates venting anger, justified or not. If it is appetitive, it facilitates adopting consummate temperance, in public and private.'[112]

Good refined or trained morals and ethics, then, are a prime key or passport to eternal salvation in paradise[113] for al-Sijistānī. It is interesting to compare this dominant motif in his thought with the ideas of al-ʿĀmirī on the same subject, and we shall pass to these in a moment.

In a nutshell, al-Sijistānī in all his thought is not a great original thinker: he depends not only on his immediate philosophical environment and those Islamic and other Middle Eastern Christian philosophers who have preceded him, but also, of course, on Aristotle and Plotinus, thus conforming to a basic paradigm suggested above. Furthermore, he is a true 'son' of al-Fārābī and member of his School in his use of Platonic thought and classifications.

Al-ʿĀmirī and Knowledge

Al-ʿĀmirī's *On the Afterlife* has been described as 'a tenth-century attempt to reconcile a Greek philosophical view of the soul with Islamic doctrine on the afterlife'.[114] The fact that al-ʿĀmirī is soaked in the Greek tradition, particularly the Neoplatonic, is not in dispute.[115] Another work attributed to al-ʿĀmirī, *On Being Happy*,[116] has been characterized as possessing 'a strong interest in Greek ethics, particularly the *Nicomachean Ethics* and [making] abundant use of both Plato and Aristotle, with a late-Neoplatonic coloration'.[117] Different commentators have stressed different aspects of this Greek sieve through which al-ʿĀmirī filtered his ideas. For Jean-Claude Vadet 'al-ʿĀmirī est nettement, comme son milieu, néo-platonisant et pythagoricien',[118] while the *Encyclopaedia of Islam* inserts him neatly into the dual paradigm, adumbrated above, and describes his philosophy as 'a rather conventional amalgam of Neoplatonism and Aristotelianism'.[119] The pluralism of the society in which al-ʿĀmirī lived is clearly reflected in his works.[120] Yet al-ʿĀmirī's corpus is much more than a mere amalgam of Greek ideas, however much that might reflect his own milieu, and however much this aspect might be stressed by authors such as those cited above. His *On the Afterlife*, for example, is as much an extended *epistemological* discourse and it is from this point of view that this work, as well as his others, will be treated here.

Al-ʿĀmirī valued knowledge as much as any of his predecessors.[121] *On the Afterlife*, and its companion volume, *On Making Known the Virtues of Islam*,[122] are both 'directed to the religious establishment' and try 'to justify philosophy and show how it may complement the religious sciences'.[123] At the beginning of *On the Afterlife*, the Prophet Muḥammad is cited as proclaiming the abundance of knowledge while the dangers of ignorance are underlined;[124] and al-ʿĀmirī provides several definitions of knowledge. For example, 'knowledge (*al-ʿilm*) is the understanding of the thing just as it is, free of mistake and slip'.[125] Alexander is quoted as stating that '[real] knowledge (*al-ʿilm*) is identifying the cause of the known (lit. *sabab al-ʿulūm*) [and] recognizing that it *is* the cause'.[126] Above all, for al-ʿĀmirī as with Plato, there is a need to know God.[127] It is important to note, however, that in al-ʿĀmirī's thought, philosophy is bound up with action. A considerable premium is placed on the merit of work: 'Knowledge', he declares, 'is at the heart of [or foundation for] work' (*al-ʿilm mabda' li 'l-ʿamal*) and 'work is the perfection of knowledge' (*al-ʿamal tamām al-ʿilm*). He continues: '*Superior knowledge* (al-ʿulūm al-fāḍila) *is only wanted for the sake of virtuous actions* (al-aʿmāl al-ṣāliḥa).'[128] Here, then, is the clearest statement by al-ʿĀmirī that he considers that knowledge is a foundation and source for ethical action, and that the two are ineluctably linked. As he puts it elsewhere: 'He who attains real wisdom (*al-ḥikma al-ḥaqīqa*) and practises true service and devotion is described as virtuous absolutely; but he who is not wise and devout can only be described as having virtue like a shadow or an image.'[129]

In *On the Afterlife*, al-ʿĀmirī identifies four categories of people according to their respective epistemological stances (*abwāb al-maʿārif*):

1 There are those who believe that that which can be perceived by the senses (*al-mudrak al-ḥissī*) has reality (*ḥaqīqa*) but deny any reality to the intellectual concept (*al-mutaṣawwar al-ʿaqlī*);
2 there are those who believe the reverse;
3 there are those who believe that neither the sensory nor the intellectual have reality; and
4 finally, there are those who believe that both have reality.[130]

For his part, al-ʿĀmirī concludes by coming down on the side of the last category: both the sensory and the intellectual have a genuine reality.[131]

On Making Known the Virtues of Islam provides a further insight into the way in which al-ʿĀmirī viewed the whole subject of knowledge (*al-ʿilm*). He divided it into the two main types: religious (*al-millī*) and philosophical (*al-ḥikmī*). Religious knowledge was further divisible into *ḥadīth* (dependent on the senses), theology (dependent on the intellect) and jurisprudence (dependent on both the senses and the intellect). All three could be serviced by linguistics (*sināʿat al-lugha*). Philosophical knowledge was also divisible into three parts: the first was physics or natural science (dependent on the senses), the second was metaphysics (dependent on the intellect), and the third was mathematics (dependent on both the senses and the intellect). Logic was the tool which serviced these three aspects of philosophical knowledge.[132] Further subdivision occurred as well[133] (see Figure 4). Al-ʿĀmiri stressed that logic was a primary tool in the achievement of real knowledge; and a Fārābian awareness of this pervades his whole thinking:

> Logic is an intellectual instrument, which alone properly enables the rational soul to distinguish between truth and untruth in speculative problems and between good and evil in practical problems. One can roughly compare the use of this instrument with that of a gauge with which one measures

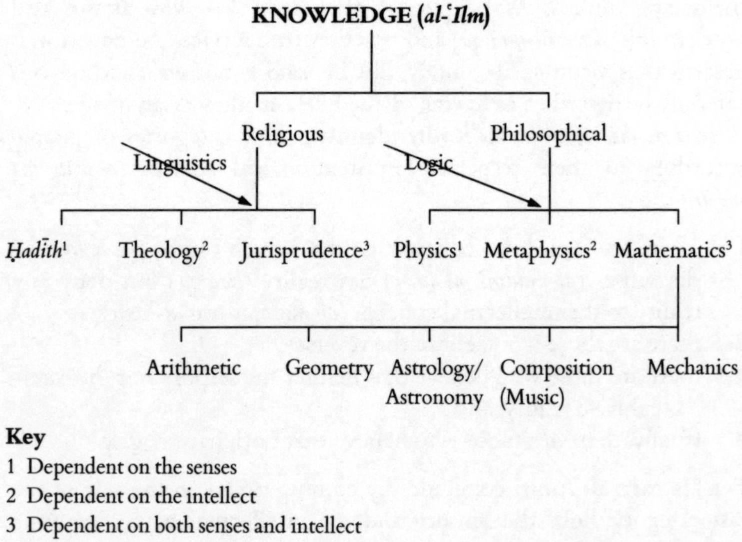

Figure 4 Al-ʿĀmiri's basic classification of knowledge in his book *On Making Known the Virtues of Islam* (*Kitāb al-Iʿlām bi Manāqib al-Islām*)

> objects of knowledge. Logic controls question and answer as well as contradiction, contrast and fallacy. It helps to resolve doubts, expose misleading statements and support other ideas which may serve to verify claims that have been raised. Besides, it also confers an intellectual pleasure, which provides a cheerful calm in matters of cognition to such an extent that the soul by itself becomes a propagandist for the acquisition of philosophy (*al-ḥikma*), not in order to earn the praise of friends thereby, but in order to be blessed with the realization of truth and the joy of certainty.[134]

In a stimulating, erudite and wide-ranging article,[135] Professor Mohammed Arkoun stresses that *On Making Known the Virtues of Islam* operates within, or employs, a lexicon and cultural paradigm which is already well established.[136] It is clearly a lexicon which gives a certain primacy to the noetic in its technical aspects.[137] Reason, however, does not conflict with revelation but complements it.[138] There is, too, a scale of values: despite the value of the rational sciences, they have a lesser nobility than the religious sciences; knowledge has an inferior position with regard to action; the former statement is a result of the latter, according to al-ʿĀmirī.[139]

In his recognition of the limitations of the human intellect,[140] he clearly seems to embrace, in part at least, the old medieval western saw which considered philosophy to be the handmaiden of theology. Or, as Rowson perhaps better states it:

> It would appear that al-ʿĀmirī agrees with al-Kindī in conceding crucial dogmatic points to Islam, but pushes his philosophical interpretations of them as far as he can; to avoid collision, he appeals in the end to the limitations of the human intellect, and the impossibility of grasping the *kayfīyāt* of the transcendent: a philosophical *bilā kayf*.[141]

Rowson goes on to maintain that such a stance set al-ʿĀmirī apart from his fellow contemporary philosophers: in particular, he differed from them 'in being actively interested in resolving the conflict with the *ʿulamā'* and winning their approval of philosophy'.[142] Above all, a clear link, as we have already seen, was established by al-ʿĀmirī between virtue and knowledge.

In conclusion, it is clear that al-ʿĀmirī, to take up once again Arkoun's point, operates within an already well-established lexical and cultural paradigm. The basic elements in this are the familiar triad of Platonism, Aristotelianism and Neoplatonism. From an epistemological point of view, al-ʿĀmirī's Platonic suspicion of knowledge yielded by sensory perception is significant:

> The eternal truths (*al-ʿulūm al-ḥaqīqiyya*) which are known with certainty – such as our belief that things equal to one thing are equal to each other, and that the whole is greater than its part – these are not established by bodily sense, *which is liable to error and inadvertence.* Rather, they are acquired by the innate (*gharīzī*) intellect, which is a divine proof, having the same relationship to the soul as the visual power has to the corporeal eye.[143]

And knowledge acquired by the rational soul is of more value and significance than that perceived by the sensual spirit.[144]

There is an epistemological dimension to the Neoplatonic substrate of *On the Afterlife* as well. One of the key Neoplatonic features of this text is the intermediate role allocated to the intellect. We have just noted that eternal truths are acquired by the innate intellect (*al-ʿaql al-gharīzī*). Certain men have had their substances blessed with 'the light of the intellect' (*nūr al-ʿaql*) which enables those men to be God's *khalīfa* on earth and make progress towards paradise.[145] As Rowson points out: 'The virtuous soul's ascent ... in terms of closeness to God ... by means of the intellect ... is thoroughly Neoplatonic.'[146] What we have in effect here, behind this text, is the great brooding image of the Universal Intellect looking up towards God in classical fashion, and downwards towards man, emanating and bequeathing that knowledge which facilitates and even precipitates virtuous action. An epistemological circle of virtue and knowledge is thus produced, and closed, whereby intellect 'looks down' from the supreme source of salvation to man, who is thus endowed with knowledge sufficient to engender a scheme or code of good ethics whose pursuit in virtuous action will lead that man to ultimate salvation.[147] Salvation is thus born of salvation's source, *via the intellect.*

Third, and finally, if we turn to the Aristotelian element of the three-part paradigm enunciated above, this too will be seen to have its epistemological dimension. In his work *On the Afterlife*, at least, al-ʿĀmirī divides the human soul into the Rational (*Nuṭqiyya*) and the Sensual (*Ḥissiyya*), and Rowson notes that the philosopher's source for his analysis of the soul here 'is Aristotle's *De Anima*, as interpreted in the late Greek Neoplatonic Schools'.[148]

If we now compare these three aspects of al-ʿĀmirī's thought – the Platonic, the Aristotelian and the Neoplatonic – (while acknowledging that there are others as well) with the same three as they appear, for example, in the thought of al-Fārābī and al-Sijistānī, we find that Arkoun's point about a common linguistic and philosophical heritage is well borne out in many respects. Above all, we are perhaps now in a position to enunciate for the first time in this volume the major underlying paradigm to which the thought of al-ʿĀmirī (as much as that of his predecessors) conforms; it may be presented succinctly, though non-exclusively, as follows: *the impact of Islamic (or Christian) dogma together with any combination of the thought of Plato, Aristotle and Plotinus on al-Fārābī and his School produced what I will term here a 'fundamental epistemology of salvation' whose primary elements were the noetic, the ethical and the soteriological.* It remains only to demonstrate in conclusion how the thought of al-Tawḥīdī also conformed to this basic paradigm.

Al-Tawḥīdī and Knowledge

Joel Kraemer, in his erudite and indispensable volume, *Humanism in the Renaissance of Islam*, neatly characterizes several of the 'Scholars, Patrons and Potentates' with whom he deals by a single epithet: thus al-ʿĀmirī, whom we have just surveyed, is 'The Philosopher'; Miskawayh becomes 'The Courtier'; and Abū Ḥayyān al-Tawḥīdī, whose attitudes towards knowledge and general epistemology will be the focus of this section, is designated 'The Secretary'.[149]

The implicit stress is correct. By virtue of his calling as 'a professional scribe, secretary, and courtier',[150] al-Tawḥīdī was enabled to write such entertaining philosophical works as *The Book of Pleasure and Conviviality*. His encyclopaedism has been much noted.[151] Indeed, the latter work, while admittedly employing a more personal and person-centred presentation than the *Epistles* (*Rasā'il*) of the Ikhwān al-Ṣafā', none the less has much in common with those *Epistles*: both are profoundly encyclopaedic in scope; both appear to be the product of philosophical and literary seminars;[152] and, if we accept the account and evidence of Abbas Hamdani, the similarities between the *Epistles* of the Ikhwān and al-Tawḥīdī's *Book of Pleasure and Conviviality* should come as no surprise. Whatever the truth or otherwise of al-Tawḥīdī's statement in which he 'named four specific contemporary writers as the authors of the otherwise anonymous encyclopedic work *Rasā'il Ikhwān al-Ṣafā*'',[153] it is clear that he had some familiarity with these *Epistles*.[154] As Hamdani notes:

At another place in his *al-Imtā'*, Abū Ḥayyān gives a long story about a Zoroastrian and a Jew as related (*ḥaddathanī*) to him by al-Qāḍī Abū 'l-Ḥasan 'Alī b. Hārūn al-Zanjānī, who is described as the *ṣāḥib al-madhhab* (leader of the sect, meaning the Qarmaṭian or the Fāṭimid). This al-Zanjānī was mentioned before as a member of the heretical group of Baṣra. The story is found verbatim in the *Rasā'il*.... Stern contends that Abū Ḥayyān, at the time of reproducing a verbal narration in his *al-Imtā'*, refreshed his memory from a copy of the *Rasā'il* itself.[155]

Furthermore, just as the *Epistles* of the Ikhwān devote a substantial section to animals and their kinds[156] (clearly written within or reflecting the Aristotelian tradition of *Historia Animalium, De Partibus Animalium* and *De Generatione Animalium*),[157] so too al-Tawḥīdī, in his *Book of Pleasure and Conviviality*, has a substantial zoological section.[158] Of course, the author was no more a professional zoologist than the Ikhwān, but he regarded such matters as part of a good education and also as observable and demonstrable aspects of God's power and wisdom.[159] There is no doubt that behind both the zoology of the Ikhwān and that of al-Tawḥīdī, a clear theological and epistemological purpose resides: God's knowledge, wisdom and power produce manifold earthly signs – such as the animals – in order that man may recognize and *know* the manifold nature of God's knowledge, wisdom and power and, acting logically, be sufficiently impressed to worship the Creator.[160] Like the Ikhwān with their *Epistles*, al-Tawḥīdī too, adheres to an Aristotelian tradition in his zoological writings, most probably drawing *inter alia* on an Arabic translation or paraphrase of Aristotle's *Historia Animalium*.[161]

The above brief survey, besides illustrating points held in common between the Ikhwān's *Epistles* and al-Tawḥīdī's *Book of Pleasure and Conviviality* (most notably and significantly for our interests, their encyclopaedic approach to, and veneration for, knowledge), also underlines the fundamental Aristotelianism at the heart of both texts. Yet this is, of course, only half the story. The Ikhwān al-Ṣafā' were profoundly Neoplatonic as well, and there was a similar orientation in al-Tawḥīdī which scholars have commented upon. For example, Kraemer points out that he was 'attracted to the Neoplatonism and Neoaristotelianism of Sijistānī and his circle'.[162] *The Encyclopaedia of Islam* notes that 'He was obviously impressed by Abū Sulaymān's Neoplatonic system, which the latter shared with most of the other contemporary Baghdad philosophers.'[163]

In summary, then, what has to be borne in mind in any assessment of al-Tawḥīdī's attitudes to knowledge and his basic epistemology is that they are underpinned by three principal factors: a devotion to encyclopaedism, a fundamental Aristotelianism and an attraction towards Neoplatonism. Though his deployment of these may not be particularly original,[164] though his intellectual honesty may sometimes be called into question,[165] and though he might treat his subjects in a somewhat unsystematic or even disorganized fashion,[166] it has also been said of him that he 'appears to have been dominated by a rare desire to achieve intellectual independence, and the ideas he put on paper are the result of much searching meditation'.[167] It is in the light of this last statement that we will try to evaluate his attitudes to knowledge and the general structure of his epistemology. And if it is rightly perceived that, for an analysis of the latter, such works as *The Book of Pleasure and Conviviality* are too disjointed and unschematic – however relevant they may be in diverse places and however much they might stress the encyclopaedic substrate to his theories of knowledge – then we may easily turn, for a more coherent and systematic epistemology, to al-Tawḥīdī's *Epistle on the Sciences* (*Risāla fī 'l-ʿUlūm*).[168]

First, it will be clear from a brief look at some of al-Tawḥīdī's views on, and general definitions of, knowledge that many of them parallel or complement other views and definitions in authors whom we have previously surveyed. Thus, a random glance reveals al-Tawḥīdī maintaining that knowledge (*al-ʿilm*) is 'the perception by the Rational Soul of things as they really are',[169] while wisdom (*al-ḥikma*) in a following definition is 'the essence of knowledge about eternal things'.[170] There is an interesting implied contrast here which seems to associate knowledge (*ʿilm*) with *this* life and wisdom (*ḥikma*) with the next. Al-Tawḥīdī also makes full use of the obvious images which may be drawn from nature: thus 'the intellect is the tree whose root is knowledge, whose branch is action, and whose fruit is the law (*sunnah*)'.[171] And knowledge, of course, may be manifest in many different, indeed, almost unexpected ways – at least, from the point of view of the epistemologist. Thus 'handwriting is the garden of knowledge'[172] and 'jewelry fashioned by the hand from the pure gold of the intellect'.[173] Indeed, the pen 'is the chief of wisdom',[174] while it is 'the light of handwriting [which] makes wisdom visible'.[175] In a statement, highly significant for its linking of the pen (i.e. knowledge, wisdom), politics (i.e. action) and, thus, implicitly the whole arena of ethics, the last quotation by al-Tawḥīdī from an unnamed Greek philosopher is continued thus: 'And the skilful handling of the calamus shapes politics.'[76]

However unusual some of the metaphor may be, there is, behind it all, a basic threefold division of the soul, which we have encountered before (for example in the epistemology of Yaḥyā b. ʿAdī), and which underpins the thought of al-Tawḥīdī: the Rational Soul, the Passionate Soul and the Appetitive or Carnal Soul.[177] The other pillar, of course, upon which al-Tawḥīdī leans is Aristotle, and this is particularly apparent in al-Tawḥīdī's devotion to logic.[178] The joy of knowledge, and that primary aspect or tool of knowledge, logic, set man apart from the animals.[179] But hubris should not be allowed to lead the scholar to desecrate his unique intellectual gifts, nor stupidity be allowed to lead the pious but stupid man to do harm by spreading his ignorance. Citing al-Tawḥīdī,[180] Rosenthal notes a warning

> against men who were pious but at the same time stupid. Together with wicked scholars, they belonged to the most harmful type of human beings. In the case of wicked scholars, knowledge suffered harm, because their knowledge was sure to be rejected on account of their wickedness. In the case of those who were pious and stupid, the harm was done through the spread of ignorance, since their piety was sure to make people accept their ignorance. Moderation in both directions was ... what promised the best hope for future salvation.[181]

It is clear from all this that, once again, the stress is on the salvific dimension of knowledge and we will return to that point later in this section. Meanwhile, we might simply note here the recurrence of another familiar theme: philosophy (a system of reason and knowledge) is still the handmaiden of, and subordinate to, theology (a system for salvation) and revelation. As al-Tawḥīdī neatly puts it: 'The prophet is above the philosopher, and the philosopher is less than the prophet. The philosopher must follow the prophet rather than vice versa, because the prophet is one who has been sent (*mabʿūth*).'[182] Reason is thus inferior to revelation, though no one can and should deny the very real links between philosophy and religion.[183]

For a slightly more systematic, though by no means complete, approach to epistemology, and some sense of what a coherent general structure or framework of knowledge might have looked like to al-Tawḥīdī, we turn now to a consideration of that author's *Epistle on the Sciences* (*Risāla fī l-ʿUlūm*).

The contemporary intellectual life of the Islam of the fourth *Hijrī* century, with all its squabbles and intellectual controversies, is clearly reflected in the work of al-Tawḥīdī.[184] And al-Tawḥīdī prints his own personality on every text. This is as true of the *Epistle on the Sciences* as it is of every other. He shows that he has a specific purpose in writing the *Epistle*: it is to record his basic and profound intellectual objection to the artificial separation of certain disciplines: Logic and Jurisprudence, Philosophy and Religion, Wisdom and Law (lit. *aḥkām*).[185] The *Epistle* encapsulates, and briefly surveys, some of the branches of the knowledge of the day under the following headings: Jurisprudence, the Qur'ān, the Traditions, Reasoning by Analogy (*Qiyās*), Scholastic Theology (*Kalām*), Grammar, Language, Logic, Medicine, Astronomy and Astrology, Arithmetic, Geometry, Rhetoric and Islamic Mysticism (*Taṣawwuf*).[186] Al-Tawḥīdī specifically states his intention to be concise and that he will not attempt to cover everything.[187] It is, therefore, a rather simpler scheme which he presents, by contrast with those of other well-known classifiers of the sciences in Arabic thought.[188] And, as Marc Bergé stresses, its omissions – History, Physics, Zoology, Music, Ethics and Politics, for example – are serious.[189] Yet, despite its lack of a logical order in the subjects treated, al-Tawḥīdī's *Epistle on the Sciences* is worthy of some attention and study.[190] And while we may agree with Bergé's final designation of it as a work of *adab*,[191] this should not prevent us from appreciating its epistemological dimensions, simple and unstructured as these may be, some of which will be highlighted in what follows.

After the opening remarks, several of which stress the very real isolation felt by the author in his present milieu, al-Tawḥīdī swiftly manifests his dislike of the man who denigrates logic.[192] He then moves to a delineation of the various branches of knowledge outlined above: aspects of jurisprudence include the permitted and the forbidden; the most difficult feature of tradition study is to distinguish the sound (*ṣaḥīḥ*) from the 'sick' (*saqīm*). After the Qur'ān and tradition, reasoning by analogy constitutes a primary crutch and handle in jurisprudence.[193] None of this is particularly remarkable. But al-Tawḥīdī goes on to emphasize, in what must be regarded as the central section of his *Epistle*, the primary role of reason in all branches of knowledge, and the necessary usages of logic (*al-manṭiq*). Logic allows ideas expressed in discourse to be considered from a whole variety of perspectives and possibilities. It can help in distinguishing a genuine proof from a doubtful one and can eliminate specious arguments.[194] It is clear, therefore, that with al-Tawḥīdī, logic should underpin the consideration of every branch of knowledge, though al-Tawḥīdī is keenly aware of the limitations of both knowledge and man.[195] If one were to attempt an answer here, on the basis of the *Epistle on the Sciences*, to the primary epistemological questions of 'What can be known?' and 'How can it be known?', one would have to reply by referring the reader to the categories of knowledge which are surveyed in the *Epistle*, in answer to the first question, and to the domain of logic as an answer to the second. But, as al-Tawḥīdī himself implies, the *Epistle on the Sciences* is by no means a complete epistemology. To formulate such a scheme of knowledge and gain a more complete picture, one needs to combine the data from this *Epistle* with that gleaned from some of his other works, surveyed above. We recall, for example, that there is still a hierarchy of values in knowledge itself, however much logic is vaunted, and that the prophet ranks above the philosopher. What the *Epistle on the Sciences* does, self-confessedly imperfectly, is to present a series of branches of knowledge, in an albeit simple, largely unstructured fashion, as part of a literary argument in favour of the merits of reason and logic, rather than a highly complex theory of intellection. The *Epistle on the Sciences* remains an *approach* towards epistemology but never a fully fledged epistemology in its own right in the sense, for example, of al-Fārābī's *Epistle on the Intellect* which we have examined in a previous chapter. Kraemer has noted of al-Tawḥīdī that he 'embraced *adab* in the broad humanistic sense'.[196] This is certainly true of the Tawḥīdī revealed to us by the *Epistle on the Sciences*.

In our assessment of al-Tawḥīdī, it remains only to examine the ethical dimension of his view of knowledge. We have already noted the lack of a section in the *Epistle on the Sciences* to deal with either ethics or politics; and it is thus clear that the ethical aspects of al-Tawḥīdī's epistemology must be sought elsewhere.

There are a variety of statements which help us to formulate a coherent view. For example, knowledge is the nourishment of the soul;[197] and just as Islam acknowledges the joint efficacy of both faith *and works* in the achievement of salvation, so al-Tawḥīdī stresses that 'action (*fiʿl*) is the source of knowledge'.[198] Above all, reason (*al-ʿaql*) is the line of communication or contact (*al-wuṣla*) between God and man,[199] as well as the arbiter between the jinn and man;[200] its *wazīr* is knowledge (*al-ʿilm*) and, by it, the servants of God are spared His punishment.[201] There could be no clearer statement that reason, the intellect, is a most significant guide to the achievement of eternal salvation and bliss. All this is confirmed elsewhere in al-Tawḥīdī's treatise, in which he deals with the art of penmanship; we have drawn upon this treatise already:[202] '"Abbās said: "... The intellect is the tongue of good actions and qualities. And good actions and qualities are the perfection of man."'[203]

In the end, then, it is clear that al-Tawḥīdī too conforms to the paradigm, adumbrated above at the end of the section dealing with al-ʿĀmirī, and contributed by his thought towards the 'fundamental epistemology of salvation' which we have identified as a major characteristic of Fārābism. Al-Tawḥīdī's writings may have fallen much more within the *adab* tradition than those of some of the other members of the School of Fārābī. We have already noted how his most famous work, *The Book of Pleasure and Conviviality*, has been described as 'a kind of philosophical *Arabian Nights*'.[204] Within the set framework of a sequence of 'nights',

> each chapter outwardly appears to sum up the discussion which had taken place at one meeting ... [and] each chapter begins with a short prelude in which the vizier usually suggests the topic to be discussed or puts a question to the author. In some cases a lively discussion ensues, in others the whole 'Night' or its greater part is taken up by the continuous discourse of the author, which, in several instances, had previously been prepared in writing. Towards the end the vizier usually asks Abū Ḥayyān to close the meeting with a 'farewell titbit' which is, as a rule, an anecdote or poem.[205]

Structurally, it is clear that al-Tawḥīdī's work has something in common with the *Arabian Nights*, with the same adherence to a frame of 'nights', though the briefest of readings will confirm that both works are very different in *content*.[206] Both belong broadly, and in their different ways, to the *adab* genre of Arabic literature.[207] And, as we saw a little earlier, al-Tawḥīdī's *Epistle on the Sciences* was also characterized by Bergé as a work of *adab*. How, then, should we conclude with regard to the epistemological dimension of al-Tawḥīdī? Basically, he was an encyclopaedic belletrist, an *adīb*, as the Arabic would put it, in the often randomly organized manner of an al-Jāḥiẓ (*c*. AD 776–868/9), whom he admired.[208] Yet al-Tawḥīdī's scattered remarks about reason and knowledge, only rarely gathered in a single work like the *Epistle on the Sciences*, are important for the light which they shed on al-Tawḥīdī's intellectual milieu generally, and the soteriology of that milieu and the School of Fārābī in particular. Perhaps it is not too ponderous to describe al-Tawḥīdī as an exponent of epistemological *adab*, at least in so far as his remarks on reason and knowledge are concerned.

4

CONCLUSION

The previous chapters have surveyed the epistemology of a number of key thinkers from the Age of Fārābism, seeking always to identify in their thought a view of *what* can be known and *how* it can be known. These were earlier identified as two of the most basic epistemological questions which can be asked. It is instructive at this point to conclude by trying to place the data of Fārābist epistemology thus garnered into some kind of brief chronological context, looking both backwards at the ideas of Plato and Aristotle, and forwards to theories produced in our own age.

Plato's earlier work, at least, 'did not clearly distinguish between *what exists* and *what is true*'. He did not subscribe to 'a propositional view of knowledge' but preferred

> to think of knowledge as a relation between a knower and a *thing*, the thing being not a proposition but rather the thing denoted by the subject of the 'that'-clause or the indirect question, as in 'I know Meno, who he is', or 'I know Meno, that he is rich' or '... whether he is rich'.

Plato also uses in his epistemology 'the model of what is now often called "knowledge by acquaintance"'.[1] Plato sought definitions and his doctrine of eternal *Ideas* thus invaded his epistemology as Hare succinctly shows: 'Plato thought that the thing about which the question was asked was an eternally existing entity, an Idea, and that the definition was a description of this entity. It is doubtful whether Socrates thought this, and Aristotle did not.'[2]

The ethical dimension also infused Plato's epistemology, and this is of considerable significance for our survey of the philosophers covered in this volume. Hare, drawing attention to the role of 'the Good' in Plato's thought, reminds us that in the *Republic*, the Good is 'the greatest thing we have to learn (505a)'.[3] In other words, the epistemological paradigm to be drawn out of all this is that to know the being of something properly, one must know 'the goodness or perfection of a good thing of that kind'. Thus, *real* knowledge of an animal or a square, man or a circle, involves knowledge of what it means to be the perfect or good exemplar of those.[4]

There is, of course, abundant scope for confusion here, particularly with respect to our definition of such emotive words as 'good' and 'perfect'.[5] But what cannot be disputed is that, by underpinning the whole framework of knowledge with such vocabulary and such concepts, Plato at least provides a point of departure for the development of an ethics-based, or ethics-infused, epistemology. The point was seized with relish in a multitude of ways by the Middle Eastern philosophers and thinkers whom we have just surveyed. And if we finally note, and add to what has preceded, Plato's well-known distrust of the evidence of sensory perception,[6] we are moving some way towards establishing part of the Platonic heritage, diverse and sometimes garbled as it was in a Middle Eastern milieu (like many another thought system), which our philosophers inherited, and on which they often drew.

However, let me stress here, as I have done elsewhere, that none of this is to imply that their philosophies were merely those of the Greeks or the west written in another script. Influence there was, and this was acknowledged by the Middle Eastern philosophers themselves. But the sacred texts which underpinned their writings, even if only as a point of departure, ensured that they were much more than erudite clones of Pythagoras, Plato, Aristotle and Plotinus. And the paradigm which we adumbrated above in chapter 3, at the end of the section on al-ʿĀmirī, began with a reference to the role of 'native' dogma and concluded with reference to that dogma's part in the production of a doctrine of salvation. There is clearly a delicate balance to be struck and the fact that we have insisted so frequently in this volume on the Greek impact on the philosophers studied should not be allowed to mislead the reader into thinking that this is the *only* dimension of their thought. This volume therefore rejects the old 'Orientalist' paradigm which saw Islamic philosophy as nothing more than an amalgam of Greek thought and denied the seminal role of Islam itself.

Aristotle agreed with Plato in perceiving links between the essence of something 'and the perfection of that thing, the end to which its whole development is striving (in Aristotle's terms, between the formal and the final cause)'.[7] This is by no means to say, of course, that Aristotle's epistemology always paralleled that of Plato. He rejected, for example, Plato's doctrine of Forms or Ideas.[8] But, like Plato, he linked knowledge and explanation. He sought a 'systematic and unified' body of knowledge whose guiding star was logic.[9] Here again, in the emphasis on logic, is a feature taken up and cherished by the philosophers covered in this book and, indeed, many others before and after them. Aristotle's major division of knowledge embraced the theoretical, practical and productive. The first included both theology and mathematics; the second, of particular significance for this book, embraced both ethics and politics; while the productive constituted such branches of knowledge as art and rhetoric.[10] Barnes identifies Aristotle as 'a self-conscious systematiser';[11] as such he prefigures many of the authors whose schemes of knowledge have been surveyed above.

For Aristotle, it is clear that knowledge is at the root of both ethics and politics which, together, form a simple endeavour; and his written works on the two subjects *demonstrate* rather than *theorize about* practical knowledge.[12] Furthermore, without a systematic accumulation and comparative study of the evidence, one will clearly not advance very far in the fields of either ethics or politics, at least as far as the scholarly study of these is concerned. As Everson puts it: 'The *Politics* is informed throughout . . . by references to the constitutions of existing states and it is evident that Aristotle regarded the analysis of the constitutions which he had collected and consideration of them in the light of the political developments in their respective states as a necessary step to any realistic constitutional theory.'[13]

Such then are what might be termed some of the main lines of epistemological development in the thought of Plato and Aristotle. Both, in a very real sense – in particular, the epistemological – are godfathers to the Age of Fārābism. If we move briefly now to our own age, some of the diverse facets of which could scarcely have been imagined by the authors covered in this volume, we find that, from the epistemological point of view, and hardly surprisingly, things have moved on since Plato. Where rationalists like the latter, and, indeed Descartes after him, 'argued that ideas of reason intrinsic to the mind are the only source of knowledge', the empirical school, epitomized in such figures as Locke and Hume, 'argued that sense experience is the primary source of our ideas, and hence of knowledge'.[14] Kant, in his epistemology, was 'anti-empiricist in denying that all knowledge is *derived* from experience' but he also opposed

Plato regarding the actual *scope* of knowledge: 'For while Plato considered true knowledge to be confined to the suprasensible world of the Forms or Ideas, Kant insisted, with the empiricists, that knowledge is limited to the world of experience.'[15]

Modern epistemology has become less concerned with scepticism, and philosophers like Wittgenstein and G.E. Moore have concentrated more on 'redirecting philosophical attention from the defence of claims to knowledge against doubt to the analysis of their meaning'.[16] And we have already referred in an earlier chapter to A.J. Ayer and his verification principle, or 'criterion of meaningfulness', whereby 'the meaning of a proposition consists in the method of its verification, that is in whatever observations or experiences show, whether or not it is true'.[17] Since the 1940s, in America and Britain, the definitional and analytical aspects of theory of knowledge, as opposed, for example, to the larger debate about scepticism, have commanded considerable, indeed massive, attention. This aspect of epistemology, says T. Sorell, 'has taken on a life of its own in the last twenty years, mainly in articles in the professional journals'.[18] He cites the example of the 1963 paper by the American philosopher Edmund L. Gettier entitled 'Is justified true belief knowledge?' This paper 'takes up a philosophically attractive analysis of factual knowledge – a statement of necessary and sufficient conditions for knowing that – and shows by counter-example that it is inadequate'.[19] Other philosophers, aware of the revision of geometry and logic in the light of quantum physics, have cast doubt 'on the whole category of the *a priori*-knowledge independent and prior to experience'.[20]

It is a cliché that fashions in philosophical thought and analysis change, and this is as true of epistemology as it is of every other field. What is clear, however – and this, of necessity, sets so much of modern epistemology apart from its medieval Islamic and Christian counterparts – is that a great deal of what is written today concerning the theory of knowledge is secular rather than religious based. I am not, however, denying a role to those whose epistemology *may* be underpinned by religion, but am simply making a general observation. As a consequence of this, epistemology loses its soteriological dimension. The Janus-faced Aristotelian model of practical knowledge, whose one side, as we have seen, is ethics, and whose other is politics, is underpinned by an epistemology where the primary 'soteriological' aspect is salvation through or in happiness (*eudaimonía*)[21] in *this* world. The epistemology of the Middle Eastern philosophers whom we have surveyed in this book on the other hand, which underpins, permeates and combines their ethics and their politics, leads to salvation in the *next* world if the theory is followed. Of course, the practical and political reality often failed to mirror any ethical, epistemological or political theory or ideal. Knowledge, and a theory of knowledge, as we have demonstrated from the preceding analysis of the thought of our five thinkers, was both possible and necessary. Islamic and Middle Eastern epistemology may have been infused with – perhaps sometimes constrained by – a theological dimension, but it was just as sophisticated and various within its chosen parameters (Qur'ānic and Greek) as much modern secular epistemology. Fārābist epistemology, like many of its western medieval counterparts, stands as a bridge between the sensory suspicions of a Plato and the analytical preoccupations of the modern age. For this reason alone, the thought of *al-Fārābī and his School* is eminently worthy of study. This book has sought to provide an introduction – and an introduction only - to that thought by using one particular aspect of it, the epistemological, as a primary focus or sieve. There are many other, equally valuable aspects waiting for the reader to discover, survey and analyse.[22] What I hope *will* be clear from all of what has been said above is that De Boer's profoundly negative and belittling remarks were somewhat wide of the mark. De Boer, writing in 1903, believed that 'Farabi had no great following of disciples' and that 'the logical tendency of Farabi passed into a philosophy of words' as far as the circle of such men as al-Sijistānī was concerned.[23] But, as this volume has tried to show, the thought of al-Sijistānī, and indeed that of all the members of the School of al-Fārābi, while not necessarily profoundly or outstandingly original, was rather more than mere 'clever conversation'[24] articulated through an Aristotelian or Neoplatonic microphone.

5

BIBLIOGRAPHICAL GUIDE

Some introductory reading is necessary in the general fields of Islamic philosophy on the one hand, and epistemology on the other, before plunging into further study of the authors surveyed in this book. Several good introductions to the field of Islamic philosophy are available of which, perhaps, Watt's *Islamic Philosophy and Theology* (2nd edn; full bibliographical details of this and all books cited in this section will be found in the Bibliography) is the easiest and most accessible to the general reader. For a deeper and more comprehensive survey, Fakhry's *A History of Islamic Philosophy* (2nd edn) will prove invaluable. Leaman's *Introduction to Medieval Islamic Philosophy* provides a fascinating insight into some of the problems which arose in that field, like the problems of creation, causality and reason versus revelation; while Netton's *Allāh Transcendent* provides both an in-depth study of the thought of some of the major philosophers of the Islamic Middle Ages and an attempt to strain that thought through a semiotic, structuralist and post-structuralist sieve, in the light of modern literary theory.

There are many books to be found on the general field of epistemology. The reader might usefully begin with Pears' brief but thought-provoking *What is Knowledge?* before moving to a more thorough treatment of the subject in such works as the excellent *Introduction to the Theory of Knowledge* by O'Connor and Carr. Other surveys of various branches of the field are to be found in the much-praised *An Encyclopaedia of Philosophy*, edited by Parkinson, while, for specifically contemporary epistemology, the reader is directed to Dancy's *An Introduction to Contemporary Epistemology.* The Greek background is well covered in Everson (ed.), *Epistemology*, in the Cambridge Companions to Ancient Thought series, which contains a selection of critical essays surveying and evaluating the field of epistemology in ancient times.

After such preliminaries, the reader will wish to bring together more closely the two fields of Islamic philosophy and epistemology, and this is well done in the thorough and wide-ranging survey by Franz Rosenthal entitled *Knowledge Triumphant: The Concept of Knowledge in Medieval Islam*, which constitutes a neat link between our two fields. For the cultural and political background to most of the thinkers who are surveyed in this volume, two outstanding books by Joel L. Kraemer have proved invaluable in the writing of my own work: I have acknowledged my indebtedness to these two works in a variety of places in this book in my end notes. The first is his *Humanism in the Renaissance of Islam: The Cultural Revival during the Buyid Age*, which not only sets the scene at length but surveys many of the scholars and thinkers dealt with in this book as well as the 'Schools, Circles and Societies' to which they belonged. Kraemer's second book, *Philosophy in the Renaissance of Islam: Abū Sulaymān al-Sijistānī and His Circle*, while nominally devoted to one specific thinker, al-Sijistānī (also surveyed in chapter 3 of this present book of mine), contains a plethora of information about his philosophical and political associates. The reader will thus find that both of these books by Kraemer are essential reading for placing the thinkers covered in *this* volume in their proper cultural, religious, philosophical and political contexts and milieu.

We turn now to the works of our five thinkers themselves: al-Fārābī, Yaḥyā b. ʿAdī, Abū Sulaymān al-Sijistānī, al-ʿĀmirī and al-Tawḥīdī. It is unfortunate that, with the exception of al-Fārābī's major works, much of the corpus of the above thinkers remains untranslated. Arabic-English bilingual editions are few. However, it *is* possible for the English speaking reader who lacks any Arabic to gain some flavour of their work. A useful starting point is Walzer's Arabic-English edition of al-Fārābī's *Virtuous City*, a work entitled by Walzer *Al-Farabi on the Perfect State.* This contains a full introduction, translation and commentary on the text, the major merits of Walzer's volume. (The Arabist will find the badly written and sometimes blurred Arabic text rather offputting and may wish to use another Arabic edition.) From the point of view of studies in epistemology, this can usefully be followed by a reading of Arthur Hyman's English translation of al-Fārābī's complex work on intellection, which is called 'Alfarabi: The Letter Concerning the Intellect'. The English translation mirrors the difficulty of the Arabic text.

For Abū Sulaymān al-Sijistānī, the non-Arabist is mainly dependent on such accessible background texts as Kraemer's cited above.

However, Périer has translated some of Yaḥyā b. ʿAdī's treatises into French (*Petits Traités Apologétiques de Yaḥyâ Ben ʿAdî*); Rescher and Shehadi have rendered his work on logic into English in an article entitled 'Yaḥyā ibn ʿAdī's Treatise "On the Four Scientific Questions Regarding the Art of Logic"'; and al-Takriti's *Yahya Ibn ʿAdi: A Critical Edition and Study of his Tahdhib al-Akhlaq* contains, in addition to the Arabic text of his *Refinement of Character*, an English summary of that text.

We are even better served with at least one of al-ʿĀmirī's works: Rowson has produced an excellent and thorough bilingual Arabic-English edition of the *Kitāb al-Amad ʿalā 'l-Abad*, under the title of *A Muslim Philosopher on the Soul and its Fate.* This contains a full Arabic text with facing English translation, together with a substantial introduction and commentary. By contrast, it is a matter of considerable regret that, to my knowledge, no translator has employed the same careful procedures to at least one of al-Tawḥīdī's really major texts like his great *Book of Pleasure and Conviviality.* However, the English speaker may gain some flavour of al-Tawḥīdī's *magnum opus* by glancing at Kopf's translation of a section, in an article entitled 'The Zoological Chapter of the *Kitāb al-Imtāʿ wal-Muʾānasa* of Abū Ḥayyān al-Tawḥīdī (10th century)'. This provides a fascinating insight, not only into the soirées attended by Abū Ḥayyān, but into the medieval zoology of the age. The reader might find it of interest to compare the data in this text of Abū Ḥayyān with a quite different animal text which appears in the *Epistles* (*Rasāʾil*) of the Ikhwān al-Ṣafāʾ. The latter is often referred to as 'The Debate of the Animals' and it has been magisterially translated, with full introduction and notes, by L.E. Goodman in his superb book *The Case of the Animals versus Man Before the King of the Jinn.* A quite different text of al-Tawḥīdī's has been translated by Franz Rosenthal: this is the former's little treatise on penmanship and it appears translated into English in Rosenthal's *Four Essays on Art and Literature in Islam* under the title 'Abū Ḥayyān at-Tawḥīdī on Penmanship'.

The titles mentioned and surveyed above are designed only to *introduce* the reader to the background and thought of the five thinkers covered in this volume. They are not intended to be exclusive. The respective bibliographies of several of the titles cited will clearly be of use in directing the interested reader to further relevant titles, as, of course, will the Bibliography on pp. 112–20.

NOTES

1 The Age of Fārābism

1 See al-Bayhaqī, *Tārīkh Ḥukamā' al-Islām*, p. 30; see also Dunlop, *Arab Civilization to A.D. 1500*, p. 184 and Walzer, art. 'Al-Fārābī', *EI*², vol. 2, p. 778.
2 See Madkour, *La Place d'al-Fârâbî*, p. 221; see also Netton, *Allāh Transcendent*, pp. 104ff.
3 See Gohlman, *The Life of Ibn Sina: A Critical Edition and Annotated Translation*, pp. 32–5 (facing Arabic-English text); see also Netton, *Allāh Transcendent*, pp. 112, 149ff.
4 See, for example, the major work by Gutas, *Avicenna and the Aristotelian Tradition*; see also the long chapter on Ibn Sīnā in Netton, *Allāh Transcendent*, pp. 149–202.
5 Kennedy, *The Prophet and the Age of the Caliphates*, p. 290; Shaban, *Islamic History: A New Interpretation, 2: A.D. 750–1055 (A.H. 132–448)*, pp. 166–7.
6 Lewis, *The Arabs in History*, p. 107.
7 See, for example, Walzer, *Al-Farabi on the Perfect State*, p. 5; see also Najjar, 'Fārābī's Political Philosophy and Shī'ism', *Studia Islamica*, vol. XIV (1961), pp. 57–72, and Marquet, *La Philosophie des Iḫwān al-Ṣafā'*, p. 542.
8 See Walzer, art. 'Al-Fārābī'. p. 778; Walzer, *Al-Farabi on the Perfect State*, p. 2.
9 See Gohlman, *The Life of Ibn Sina.*
10 Walzer, art. 'Al-Fārābī', p. 778.
11 'The rather lengthy biography in Ibn Khallikān's *Wafayāt al-Aʿyān* is open to criticism as regards its authenticity.' (Madkour, 'Al-Fārābī', p. 450); see also Walzer, *Al-Farabi on the Perfect State*, p. 2.
12 The principal primary sources drawn upon for the life of al-Fārābī are: al-Bayhaqī, *Tārīkh Ḥukamā' al-Islām*, pp. 30–5; Ibn Abī Uṣaybiʿa, *Kitāb ʿUyūn al-Anbā' fī Ṭabaqāt al-Aṭibbā'*, pp. 92–3, 603–9; Ibn Khallikān, *Wafayāt al-Aʿyān*, vol. 5, pp. 153–7; Ibn Ṣāʿid, *Ṭabaqāt al-Umam*, pp. 70–2; al-Masʿūdī, *Kitāb al-Tanbīh wa 'l-Ishrāf*, pp. 105–6; Ibn al-Qifṭī, *Tārīkh al-Ḥukamā'*, pp. 277–80. His life may also be briefly studied in, *inter alia*, the following secondary sources which have been consulted and used here: Badawī, *Histoire de la Philosophie en Islam*, vol. 2, pp. 478–83; Dunlop, *Arab Civilization to A.D. 1500*, pp. 184–5; Fakhry, *A History of Islamic Philosophy*, pp. 107–9; Madkour, 'Al-Fārābī', pp. 450–2; Netton, *Allāh Transcendent*, pp. 99–101; Walzer, art. 'Al-Fārābī', pp. 778–9; Walzer, *Al-Farabi on the Perfect State*, pp. 2–5.

13 See Netton, *Allāh Transcendent*, pp. 99–100.
14 Al-ʿĀmirī, *Kitāb al-Saʿāda wa 'l-Isʿād*, pp. 194, 211; Dunlop, *Arab Civilization to A.D. 1500*, pp. 184, 319 (n. 91).
15 Ibn Khallikān, *Wafayāt al-Aʿyān*, vol. 5, p. 155.
16 Madkour, 'Al-Fārābī', p. 451; see also Badawī, *Histoire de la Philosophie en Islam*, vol. 2, p. 482 and Netton, *Allāh Transcendent*, p. 100.
17 For example, see Ibn Abī Uṣaybiʿa, *Kitāb ʿUyūn al-Anbā'*, pp. 603–4; Ibn Khallikān, *Wafayāt al-Aʿyān*, vol. 5, p. 156; Ibn al-Qifṭī, *Tārīkh al-Ḥukamā'*, p. 279.
18 See Walzer, *Al-Farabi on the Perfect State*, p. 4, who observes: 'We are told that he [al-Fārābī] always wore a brown Ṣūfī garb. In al-Fārābī's day no adherence to mystical "Ṣūfī" views was indicated by the use of this garment, and in his particular case it can be easily shown that he was decidedly opposed to the mystic's unworldly interpretation of life and his overemphasis on the world to come.' Compare also the casual practices of Ibn Baṭṭūṭa, referred to in Netton, 'Myth, Miracle and Magic in the *Riḥla* of Ibn Baṭṭūṭa', *Journal of Semitic Studies*, vol. XXIX, no. 1 (Spring 1984), p. 135.
19 Ibn Abī Uṣaybiʿa, *Kitāb ʿUyūn al-Anbā'*, p. 603; Ibn Khallikān, *Wafayāt al-Aʿyān*, vol. 5, p. 156; Ibn al-Qifṭī, *Tārīkh al-Ḥukamā'*, p. 279.
20 Al-Bayhaqī, *Tārīkh Ḥukamā' al-Islām*, pp. 33–4; see also Netton, *Allāh Transcendent*, pp. 101, 137 (n. 26).
21 Ibn Khallikān, *Wafayāt al-Aʿyān*, vol. 5, p. 155. At least some of his books must have been written in Damascus: see ibid., p. 156.
22 Ibn Abī Uṣaybiʿa, *Kitāb ʿUyūn al-Anbā'*, p. 603.
23 For example, Fakhry, *History of Islamic Philosophy*, pp. 107–8; Walzer, *Al-Farabi on the Perfect State*, pp. 3–4.
24 Badawī, *Histoire de la Philosophie en Islam*, vol. 2, pp. 481–2.
25 Ibn al-Qifṭī, *Tārīkh al-Ḥukamā'*, p. 279.
26 Badawī, *Histoire de la Philosophie en Islam*, vol. 2, p. 482; Zimmermann, *Al-Farabi's Commentary and Short Treatise on Aristotle's* De Interpretatione, p. cxviii.
27 Al-Fārābī, *Kitāb al-Mūsīqā al-Kabīr*, ed. Khashaba and al-Ḥafnī. See also Dunlop, *Arab Civilization to A.D. 1500*, pp. 185–6; Walzer, *Al-Farabi on the Perfect State*, p. 438, esp. n. 640; Wright, 'Music' in Schacht and Bosworth (eds), *The Legacy of Islam*, 2nd edn, pp. 490–5.
28 Al-Bayhaqī, *Tārīkh Ḥukamā' al-Islām*, pp. 32–3; Ibn Khallikān, *Wafayāt al-Aʿyān*, vol. 5, pp. 155–6. See also Dunlop, *Arab Civilization to A.D. 1500*, pp. 185, 319 (n. 100).
29 Ibn Khallikān, *Wafayāt al-Aʿyān*, vol. 5, pp. 155–6. See also Badawī, *Histoire de la Philosophie en Islam*, vol. 2, p. 482.
30 Ikhwān al-Ṣafā', *Rasā'il*, vol. 1, pp. 185, 289; see Netton, *Muslim Neoplatonists*, p. 13.
31 See Netton, *Allāh Transcendent*, pp. 103, 129, 138 n. 44. A common source theory is supported elsewhere: see Hamdani, 'The Arrangement of the *Rasā'il Ikhwān al-Ṣafā'* and the Problem of Interpolations', *Journal of Semitic Studies*, vol. XXIX, no. 1 (Spring 1984), pp. 103, 108–9. In any case, '[Al-Fārābī's] impact on the writings of 4th/10th century authors such as the Ikhwān al-Ṣafā' ... is undeniable' (Walzer, art. 'Al-Fārābī', p. 780).
32 Ikhwān al-Ṣafā', *Rasā'il*, vol. 1, p. 185.
33 ibid., p. 289.

34 ibid., p. 185. For an alternative translation see Shiloah, *The Epistle on Music of the Ikhwan al-Safa*, p. 14.

35 Ikhwān al-Ṣafā', *Rasā'il*, vol. 1, p. 289.

36 See above, nn. 18, 25.

37 See Netton, *Allāh Transcendent*, pp. 99–148.

38 Ibn Khallikān, *Wafayāt al-A'yān*, vol. 5, p. 156; Ibn Abī Uṣaybi'a, *Kitāb 'Uyūn al-Anbā'*, p. 604.

39 Ibn Abī Uṣaybi'a, *Kitāb 'Uyūn al-Anbā'*, pp. 317–18.

40 (My italics) trans in Rosenthal, *The Classical Heritage in Islam*, pp. 22–3. For the Arabic text see Badawī (ed.), *Manṭiq Arisṭū*, pt. 3, pp. 1017–18.

41 The Arabic reads *kāna yanbahiru* and so could also mean 'he used to be dazzled' (as well as 'he used to be breathless' which I have rendered more colloquially as 'he would become laboured').

42 Al-Tawḥīdī, *Kitāb al-Imtā* 'wa 'l-Mu'ānasa, pt. 1, p. 37; Endress, *The Works of Yaḥyā ibn 'Adī*, pp. 2, 8.

43 Fakhry, *A History of Islamic Philosophy*, p. 192.

44 Samir, 'Le *Tahḏīb al-Aḫlāq* de Yaḥyā b. 'Adī (m. 974) attribué a Ǧāḥiẓ et à Ibn al-'Arabī', *Arabica*, vol. XXI (1974), p. 138.

45 For some of their names, see ibid.; see also Endress, *The Works of Yaḥyā ibn 'Adī*, pp. 8–9 and Yaḥyā b. 'Adī, *Maqāla fī 'l-Tawḥīd li-Shaykh Yaḥyā b. 'Adī*, ed. Samir, p. xi (French introd.).

46 See Endress' magisterial inventory of Yaḥyā's works in his *The Works of Yaḥyā ibn 'Adī*, which reveals the full extent of Yaḥyā's interests from Aristotelian commentary, through metaphysics and ethics, to knotty questions of philosophy and Nestorian and Monophysite theology.

47 Samir, 'Le *Tahḏīb al-Aḫlāq* de Yaḥyā b. 'Adī', p. 138.

48 See Endress, *The Works of Yaḥyā ibn 'Adī*, pp. 4–5; Yaḥyā b. 'Adī *Maqāla fī 'l-Tawḥīd*, ed. Samir, p. 25 (Arabic introd.).

49 See Ibn Abī Uṣaybi'a, *Kitāb 'Uyūn al-Anbā'*, p. 317.

50 Endress, *The Works of Yaḥyā ibn 'Adī*, pp. 5–6; Yaḥyā b. 'Adī, *Maqāla fī 'l-Tawḥīd*, ed. Samir, pp. 25–37 (Arabic introd.), x–xi (French introd.).

51 Endress, *The Works of Yaḥyā ibn 'Adī*, p. 5.

52 ibid., p. 8.

53 See ibid., pp. 6–7.

54 For further details of the life and philosophy of al-Kindī, see Netton, *Allāh Transcendent*, pp. 45–98.

55 Fakhry, *A History of Islamic Philosophy*, p. 196.

56 ibid., p. 197.

57 For the Arabic text with a French translation, see Périer, 'Un traité de Yaḥyâ ben 'Adî: Défense du dogme de la Trinité contre les objections d'al-Kindî', *Revue de l'Orient Chrétien*, no. 1, 3ᵉ sér., t. ii (=t. xxii) (1920–1), pp. 3–21. A revised translation appears in Périer (ed.), *Petits Traités Apologétiques de Yaḥyâ Ben 'Adî*, pp. 118–28. See also Endress, *The Works of Yaḥyā ibn 'Adī*, pp. 100–1; Yaḥyā b. 'Adi, *Maqāla fī 'l-Tawḥīd*, ed. Samir, p. xxix (French introd.); and Fakhry, *A History of Islamic Philosophy*, pp. 197–9.

58 Fakhry, *A History of Islamic Philosophy*, p. 192.

59 ibid., pp. 192–3. For an edition of the Arabic text, see al-Takriti, *Yahya Ibn 'Adi: A Critical Edition and Study of his Tahdhib al-Akhlaq*; see also Endress, *The Works of Yaḥyā ibn 'Adī*, pp. 82–5; Yaḥyā b. 'Adī, *Maqāla fī 'l-Tawḥīd*, ed. Samir,

pp. xxviii-xxxv (French introd.); Samir, 'Le *Tahdīb al-Aḫlāq* de Yaḥyā b. ʿAdī', pp. 111-38.

60 For these dates, see Netton, *Allāh Transcendent*, pp. 63, 92 (n. 177). These dates depend on Kraemer, 'Abû Sulaymân As-Sijistânî' (Ph.D. thesis), p. 8; Kraemer later gives slightly different dates for al-Sijistānī in his *Humanism in the Renaissance of Islam*, p. 139.

61 See Ibn Abī Uṣaybiʿa, *Kitāb ʿUyūn al-Anbā'*, p. 317.

62 ibid., p. 427; see also al-Tawḥīdī, *Kitāb al-Imtāʿ wa 'l-Mu'ānasa*, pt. 2, p. 18.

63 Ibn Abī Uṣaybiʿa, *Kitāb ʿUyūn al-Anbā'*, p. 427.

64 Al-Sijistānī, *Muntakhab*, ed. Dunlop, p. xii (English introd.); al-Sijistānī, *Muntakhab*, ed. Badawī, p. 5 (French introd.). See al-Tawḥīdī, *Kitāb al-Imtāʿ wa 'l-Mu'ānasa*, pt. 2, pp. 18, 38.

65 Kraemer, *Humanism in the Renaissance of Islam*, p. 139. Kraemer disputes the usually expressed view (see n. 52 above) that al-Sijistānī 'became head of the Baghdad school of philosophical studies after Ibn ʿAdī'.

66 Ibn al-Qifṭī, *Tārīkh al-Ḥukamā'*, p. 283; Kraemer, 'Abû Sulaymân As-Sijistânî' (Ph.D. thesis), p. 24.

67 Al-Sijistānī, *Muntakhab*, ed. Dunlop, p. xiii (English introd.).

68 ibid.

69 See al-Sijistānī, *Muntakhab*, ed. Badawī, p. 10 (French introd.).

70 Stern, art. 'Abū Sulaymān Muḥammad B. Ṭāhir B. Bahrām al-Sidjistānī al-Manṭiḳī', *EI*^{2}, vol. 1, p. 151. The statement has been challenged by Kraemer, 'Abû Sulaymân As-Sijistânî' (Ph.D. thesis), p. 4.

71 Kraemer, 'Abû Sulaymân As-Sijistânî' (Ph.D. thesis), p. 1.

72 See al-Sijistānī, *Muntakhab*, ed. Dunlop, p. ix (English introd.).

73 ibid., p. xi (English introd.).

74 Kraemer, 'Abû Sulaymân As-Sijistânî' (Ph.D. thesis), p. 4.

75 ibid., pp. 5, 310.

76 ibid., p. 311.

77 ibid., p. 310.

78 ibid. The biographical data for Abū Sulaymān al-Sijistānī which precedes has been drawn from the following primary and secondary sources, to which the reader is referred for further information: (1) al-Bayhaqī, *Tārīkh Ḥukamā' al-Islām*, pp. 82–3; Ibn Abī Uṣaybiʿa, *Kitāb ʿUyūn al-Anbā'*, pp. 91, 152, 259, 260, 427–8, 492; Ibn al-Qifṭī, *Tārīkh al-Ḥukamā'*, pp. 84, 224–5, 282–3; al-Tawḥīdī, *Kitāb al-Imtāʿ wa 'l-Mu'ānasa, passim*; (2) al-Sijistānī, *Muntakhab*, ed. Badawī pp. 3–11 (French introd.); al-Sijistānī, *Muntakhab*, ed. Dunlop, pp. x–xiii (English introd.); Kraemer, 'Abû Sulaymân As-Sijistânî' (Ph.D. thesis), *passim*; Kraemer, *Humanism in the Renaissance of Islam*, pp. 139ff.; Kraemer, *Philosophy in the Renaissance of Islam*, pp. 1–3 and *passim*; Stern, art. 'Abū Sulaymān Muḥammad B. Ṭāhir B. Bahrām al-Sidjistānī al-Manṭiḳī', pp. 151–2.

79 See Kraemer, *Humanism in the Renaissance of Islam*, p. 147; see also Ibn al-Qifṭī, *Tārīkh al-Ḥukamā'*, pp. 282–3.

80 Kraemer, *Humanism in the Renaissance of Islam*, pp. 147–8; see also p. 150. Compare Matthew 16: 25–6.

81 See above, n. 14.

82 See Walzer, art. 'Al-Fārābī', p. 780; see also Vadet, *Une Défense Philosophique de la Sunna*, pp. 15–22.

83 Vadet, 'Le Souvenir de l'Ancienne Perse chez le Philosophe Abū l-Ḥasan

al-ʿĀmirī (m. 381 H.)', *Arabica*, vol. XI (1964), p. 258.

84 Vadet, *Une Défense Philosophique de la Sunna*, p. 10.

85 ibid., p. 8.

86 Al-Tawḥīdī, *Kitāb al-Imtāʿ wa 'l-Mu'ānasa*, pt. 2, p. 84.

87 See al-Sijistānī, *Muntakhab Ṣiwān al-Ḥikma*, ed. Badawī, p. 310. The principal primary and secondary sources used in this brief survey of al-ʿĀmirī's life are the following: (1) Miskawayh, *Tajārib al-Umam*, vol. 2, p. 277; al-Sijistānī, *Muntakhab Ṣiwān al-Ḥikma*, ed. Badawī, pp. 307–10; al-Tawḥīdī, *Kitāb al-Imtāʿ wa 'l-Mu'ānasa*, pt. 1, pp. 35–6, 222–3, pt. 2, pp. 84, 88, pt. 3, pp. 91–6; al-Tawḥīdī, *al-Muqābasāt*, pp. 116, 171, 177, 340, 357; (2) Dunlop, art. 'Al-Balkhī', *EI*[2], vol. 1, p. 1003; Kraemer, *Humanism in the Renaissance of Islam*, pp. 233–41; Rowson, art. 'Al-ʿĀmirī', *EI*[2] *Supp.* Fascs 1–2, pp. 72–3; Rowson, 'Al-ʿĀmirī on the Afterlife' esp. pp. 6–10, see also pp. 31–5; Vadet, *Une Défense Philosophique de la Sunna*, pp. 7–15.

88 Rosenthal, 'State and Religion According to Abû l-Ḥasan al-ʿÂmirî', *Islamic Quarterly*, vol. 3, no. 1 (April 1956), p. 43; Rowson, 'Al-ʿĀmirī on the Afterlife', p. 10; Rowson, art. 'Al-ʿĀmirī', p. 72.

89 For the identification of the authorship, see Rowson, 'Al-ʿĀmirī on the Afterlife', pp. 21–3.

90 See the remarks of Rosenthal, 'State and Religion', p. 43, and Rowson, art. 'Al-ʿĀmirī', p. 72.

91 For the identification of al-ʿĀmirī and Abū 'l-Ḥasan b. Abī Dharr, see Kraemer, *Humanism in the Renaissance of Islam*, p. 233. See also Rowson, 'Al-ʿĀmirī on the Afterlife', pp. 21–3.

92 Arberry, 'An Arabic Treatise on Politics', *Islamic Quarterly*, vol. 2, no. 1 (April 1955), p. 22.

93 Rowson, art. 'Al-ʿĀmirī', p. 72.

94 Rowson, 'Al-ʿĀmirī on the Afterlife', p. 38.

95 Kraemer, *Humanism in the Renaissance of Islam*, p. 235 (n. 76).

96 Vadet, *Une Défense Philosophique de la Sunna*, p. 50.

97 Kraemer, *Humanism in the Renaissance of Islam*, pp. 238–9; see al-Tawḥīdī, *Kitāb al-Imtāʿ wa 'l-Mu'ānasa*, pt. 3, pp. 94–5 cited in Kraemer, *Humanism in the Renaissance of Islam*, p. 238.

98 Kraemer, *Humanism in the Renaissance of Islam*, p. 239.

99 ibid., pp. 238–9.

100 Rowson, 'Al-ʿĀmirī on the Afterlife', p. 30.

101 Ibn Khallikān, *Wafayāt al-Aʿyān*, vol. 5, p. 113; Stern, art. 'Abū Ḥayyān al-Tawḥīdī', *EI*[2], vol. 1, p. 126; Kraemer, *Humanism in the Renaissance of Islam*, p. 212.

102 Hourani, *Islamic Rationalism*, p. 6.

103 Kraemer, *Humanism in the Renaissance of Islam*, p. 215. For the *Akhlāq*, see the Bibliography.

104 Fakhry, *A History of Islamic Philosophy*, p. 183.

105 Kraemer, *Humanism in the Renaissance of Islam*, p. 216; see also Stern, art. 'Abū Ḥayyān al-Tawḥīdī', p. 127.

106 Among the principal primary and secondary sources for the life of Abū Ḥayyān al-Tawḥīdī that have been drawn upon for the brief survey above, are the following: (1) Ibn Khallikān, *Wafayāt al-Aʿyān*, vol. 5, pp. 112–13; Yāqūt, *Irshād*, vol. 5, pp. 380–407; (2) Fakhry, *A History of Islamic Philosophy*, pp. 182–5;

Kraemer, *Humanism in the Renaissance of Islam*, pp. 212–22; Mahjoub, 'Abu Hayyan at-Tawhidi: Un Rationaliste Original', *Revue de l'Institut des Belles Lettres Arabes* (Tunis), vol. 27 (1964), pp. 317–44; Stern, art. 'Abū Ḥayyān al-Tawḥīdī', pp. 126–7.

107 Kraemer, *Humanism in the Renaissance of Islam*, pp. 213, 216.
108 Stern, art. 'Abū Ḥayyān al-Tawḥīdī', p. 127.
109 Mahjoub, 'Abu Hayyan at-Tawhidi', p. 329.
110 See Kraemer, *Humanism in the Renaissance of Islam*, pp. 216, 218.
111 ibid., p. 214; Stern, art. 'Abū Ḥayyān al-Tawḥīdī', p. 126.
112 Stern, art. 'Abū Ḥayyān al-Tawḥīdī', p. 127.
113 Kraemer, *Humanism in the Renaissance of Islam*, p. 220, citing Anawati and Gardet, *Mystique Musulmane*, p. 46.
114 Kraemer, *Humanism in the Renaissance of Islam*, p. 222.
115 Mardrus and Mathers (trans.), *The Book of the Thousand Nights and One Night*, vol. 2, p. 370. See also ibid., pp. 389–90.
116 Gerhardt, *The Art of Story-Telling*, pp. 420–1. See also the initial remarks of F. Omar in his article, 'Hārūn al-Rashīd', *EI*², vol. 3, p. 232.
117 See Fakhry, *A History of Islamic Philosophy*, p. 183.
118 See Nicholson, *A Literary History of the Arabs*, p. 313.
119 Trans. Arberry, *Poems of al-Mutanabbī* (Arabic–English text), pp. 54–5; see also al-Mutanabbī, *Dīwān*, p. 261.
120 Trans. Arberry, *Poems of al-Mutanabbī*, pp. 76–7; see also al-Mutanabbī, *Dīwān*, p. 364.
121 Trans. Nicholson, *A Literary History of the Arabs*, p. 305; see al-Mutanabbī, *Dīwān*, p. 339.
122 Nicholson, *A Literary History of the Arabs*, p. 305.
123 Trans. Arberry, *Poems of al-Mutanabbī*, pp. 82–3; see also al-Mutanabbī, *Dīwān*, p. 383.
124 Nicholson, *A Literary History of the Arabs*, pp. 305–7.
125 See Ibn Abī Uṣaybiʿa, *Kitāb ʿUyūn al-Anbāʾ*, pp. 603–4.
126 Walzer, *Al-Farabi on the Perfect State*, p. 5.
127 See Netton, 'Myth, Miracle and Magic in the *Riḥla* of Ibn Baṭṭūṭa', pp. 139–40; Ibn Baṭṭūṭa, *Riḥla*, pp. 528–9.
128 Trans. Gibb, *The Travels of Ibn Baṭṭūṭa*, vol. 3, p. 750; see Ibn Baṭṭūṭa, *Riḥla*, p. 515.
129 Ibn Baṭṭūṭa, *Riḥla*, pp. 515–16.
130 For further information on the relationship between Hārūn and the Barmakid *wazīr*s and secretaries, see al-Masʿūdī, *Murūj al-Dhahab*, vol. 3, pp. 368–87; al-Ṭabarī, *Tārīkh*, vol. 8, pp. 230–364, trans. Bosworth, *The History of al-Ṭabarī: Volume XXX. The ʿAbbāsid Caliphate in Equilibrium*, pp. 91–335. See also Barthold and Sourdel, art. 'Al-Barāmika', *EI*², vol. 1, pp. 1033–36; Horovitz, art. 'ʿAbbāsa', *EI*², vol. 1, p. 14; and Omar, art. 'Hārūn al-Rashīd', pp. 232–4.
131 (My italics) Barthold and Sourdel, art. 'Al-Barāmika', p. 1035.
132 Bosworth identifies him as 'al-Faḍl b. ʿAbd al-Ṣamad, *mājin* poet of Baghdad, who died before 207 (822) and whose verses were gathered into a *dīwān* by the Barmakīs' (Bosworth, *History of al-Ṭabarī: Volume XXX*, p. 226, n. 781).
133 i.e. al-Faḍl b. Yaḥyā al-Barmakī, imprisoned by Hārūn in AD 803 (d. AD 808).
134 i.e. Jaʿfar b. Yaḥyā al-Barmakī, suddenly executed by Hārūn in AD 803.
135 i.e. Muḥammad b. Yaḥyā al-Barmakī, imprisoned by Hārūn in AD 803.

136 Trans. Bosworth, *The History of al-Ṭabarī: Volume XXX*, p. 227; for the original Arabic text see al-Ṭabarī, *Tārīkh*, vol. 8, pp. 300–1; see also al-Masʿūdī, *Murūj al-Dhahab*, vol. 3, p. 382.
137 Unidentified: see Bosworth, *The History of al-Ṭabarī: Volume XXX*, p. 228 (n. 786).
138 Trans. Bosworth, *The History of al-Ṭabarī: Volume XXX*, p. 228; for the original Arabic text, see al-Ṭabarī, *Tārīkh*, vol. 8, p. 301; see also al-Masʿūdī, *Murūj al-Dhahab*, vol. 3, p. 382.
139 Al-Masʿūdī, *Murūj al-Dhahab*, vol. 3, p. 373; Plato, *Symposium*, 191C, pp. 61–2.
140 Al-Masʿūdī, *Murūj al-Dhahab*, vol. 3, pp. 370–5: the passages have been translated in Lunde and Stone (trans. and eds), *The Meadows of Gold*, pp. 109–14. See also Meisami, 'Masʿūdī on Love and the Fall of the Barmakids', *Journal of the Royal Asiatic Society*, no. 2 (1989), pp. 252–77.
141 See Kraemer, *Humanism in the Renaissance of Islam*, p. 195.
142 Barthold and Sourdel, art. 'Al-Barāmika', p. 1034.
143 Kraemer, *Humanism in the Renaissance of Islam*, pp. 191–2.
144 ibid., p. 206.
145 Barthold and Sourdel, art. 'Al-Barāmika', p. 1035; Kraemer, *Humanism in the Renaissance of Islam*, pp. 194–5.
146 Kraemer, *Humanism in the Renaissance of Islam*, p. 87; see also p. 288.
147 ibid., p. 288.
148 ibid., p. 89; Walzer, *Al-Farabi on the Perfect State*, p. 5.
149 Canard, art. 'Ḥamdānids', *EI*[2], vol. 3, pp. 127, 129; Walzer, *Al-Farabi on the Perfect State*, pp. 5, 17.
150 Kennedy, *The Prophet and the Age of the Caliphates*, p. 277; see also pp. 278–9.
151 ibid., p. 280.
152 See ibid., p. 279.
153 Shaban, *Islamic History: A New Interpretation, 2*, p. 162; Kraemer, *Humanism in the Renaissance of Islam*, p. 288, see also pp. 40, 43.
154 Kraemer, *Humanism in the Renaissance of Islam*, p. 39; Shaban, *Islamic History: A New Interpretation, 2*, p. 162.
155 See Kraemer, *Humanism in the Renaissance of Islam*, pp. 39–43.
156 ibid., p. 41.
157 ibid., p. 43.
158 ibid., p. 280.
159 ibid., pp. 221–2.
160 ibid., pp. 262–3.
161 ibid., pp. 72–3; Hourani, *Islamic Rationalism*, p. 6.
162 Kraemer, *Humanism in the Renaissance of Islam*, p. 73.
163 See Kraemer, *Philosophy in the Renaissance of Islam*, pp. 6–24; Kraemer, *Humanism in the Renaissance of Islam*, p. 286.
164 Kraemer, *Philosophy in the Renaissance of Islam*, pp. 6 (esp. n. 15), 8; Bosworth, *The Islamic Dynasties*, p. 104.
165 Bosworth, *Sīstān under the Arabs*, p. 91.
166 I am indebted to my good friend and colleague Professor C.E. Bosworth of the University of Manchester, both for confirming this and providing much useful advice about Ṣaffārid and other sources.
167 Kraemer, *Philosophy in the Renaissance of Islam*, p. 16.
168 See Kraemer, *Humanism in the Renaissance of Islam*, p. 234.

169 ibid., pp. 87, 91, 288.
170 See ibid., p. 288.

2 The Epistemological Substrate of Fārābism (i): The Paradigm of the Second Master

1 See Robson, art. 'Ḥadīth', *EI*², vol. 3, p. 23.
2 See Netton, 'Basic Structures and Signs of Alienation in the *Riḥla* of Ibn Jubayr', *Journal of Arabic Literature*, vol. XXII (1991), pp. 21–37. See also Juynboll, *Muslim Tradition*, pp. 66–70 for 'A tentative chronology of *ṭalab al-ʿilm*'.
3 See Leavis, *The Great Tradition.*
4 See Netton, 'Arabia and the Pilgrim Paradigm of Ibn Baṭṭūṭa: A Braudelian Approach' in Netton (ed.), *Arabia and the Gulf*, pp. 29–42 and Netton, 'Myth, Miracle and Magic in the *Riḥla* of Ibn Baṭṭūṭa', pp. 131–40.
5 Robson, art. 'Al-Bukhārī, Muḥammad B. Ismāʿīl', *EI*², vol. 1, pp. 1296–7.
6 See above, n. 4.
7 For a superb and very well-organized introduction to the whole subject of knowledge in Islam, see Rosenthal, *Knowledge Triumphant.*
8 See Netton, *Muslim Neoplatonists*, pp. 16–18; Peters, *God's Created Speech*, pp. 40–3; Plato, *Phaedo*, 64B–66E in Plato, *The Last Days of Socrates*, pp. 109–12. Plato asks (p. 109) 'Then when is it that the soul attains to truth?' and then comments: 'When it tries to investigate anything with the help of the body, it is obviously led astray.'
9 L.E. Goodman and M.J. Goodman, 'Creation and Evolution: Another Round in an Ancient Struggle', *Zygon*, vol. 18, no. 1 (1983), p. 31.
10 Rosenthal, *Knowledge Triumphant*, pp. 164–5.
11 ibid., pp. 165–6.
12 ibid., p. 166.
13 ibid., p. 167; see also pp. 202–3.
14 ibid., p. 168.
15 See Marenbon, *Early Medieval Philosophy (480–1150): An Introduction*, pp. 109–10, 131–9.
16 See Staniland, *Universals, passim.*
17 See Ayer, *Language, Truth and Logic, passim.*
18 Pears, *What is Knowledge?*, p. 96.
19 ibid.
20 ibid., p. 97.
21 Flew (ed.), *A Dictionary of Philosophy*, p. 101, s.v. 'epistemology'.
22 O'Connor and Carr, *Introduction to the Theory of Knowledge*, pp. 1–2.
23 See above, n. 8.
24 Netton, *Muslim Neoplatonists*, p. 17.
25 ibid., pp. 17–18; see Ikhwān al-Ṣafāʾ, *Rasāʾil*, vol. 3, p. 424.
26 See above, n. 22.
27 See Netton, *Allāh Transcendent* for a survey of what is involved.
28 Rosenthal, *Knowledge Triumphant*, p. 195.
29 Trans. Dunlop in al-Fārābī, *Fuṣūl al-Madanī: Aphorisms of the Statesman* (ed. Dunlop), p. 43. For the original Arabic, see ibid., p. 126. See also Rosenthal, *Knowledge Triumphant*, p. 36 (n. 2).

30 Rescher, *Al-Fārābī: An Annotated Bibliography*, pp. 43–4.
31 ibid., p. 43; al-Fārābī, *Kitāb al-Ḥurūf*, p. 34 (Arabic introd.).
32 Rosenthal, *Knowledge Triumphant*, p. 195.
33 ibid.
34 See al-Rabe, 'Muslim Philosophers' Classifications of the Sciences', p. 99.
35 Rosenthal, *Knowledge Triumphant*, p. 195.
36 Al-Rabe, 'Muslim Philosophers' Classifications of the Sciences', pp. 100, 108–9; al-Fārābī, *Iḥṣā' al-ʿUlūm*, pp. 21–54 (Arabic), pp. 128–44 (Latin), pp. 13–37 (Spanish); Rescher, *Al-Fārābī: An Annotated Bibliography*, pp. 30–1.
37 Al-Rabe, 'Muslim Philosophers' Classifications of the Sciences', pp. 13, 97, 108–9.
38 ibid.
39 ibid., pp. 13, 76, 96.
40 ibid., p. 77, esp. n. 11.
41 Al-Fārābī, *Iḥṣā' al-ʿUlūm*, p. 7 (Arabic); see also p. 119 (Latin), p. 3 (Spanish).
42 ibid., pp. 8–9 (Arabic), see also pp. 119–20 (Latin), p. 4 (Spanish). Al-Rabe ('Muslim Philosophers' Classifications of the Sciences', p. 79) also espouses a similar fivefold division of al-Fārābī's comments, but he appears to avoid completely the usage of the word 'epistemology'.
43 Al-Rabe, 'Muslim Philosophers' Classifications of the Sciences', pp. 80, 15–16.
44 Al-Rabe, in ibid., p. 80, prefers to translate *al-ʿIlm al-Madani*, which I have loosely rendered here as 'Civil Science', by the term 'Political Science'. Al-Fārābī's own initial definition that '[*al-ʿIlm*] *al-Madanī* makes enquiry into the kinds of actions and intentional ways of behaviour and natural dispositions and character and traits and the natures from which those actions and ways of behaviour derive' (*Iḥṣā' al-ʿUlūm*, p. 91 (Arabic)), makes it clear, however, that his term embraces a whole range of human and social intercourse rather than what is more narrowly conveyed by the term 'political science' today, although he clearly has many aspects of today's usage in mind as well. (See, for example, *Iḥṣā' al-ʿUlūm*, p. 93 (Arabic).)
45 See al-Rabe, 'Muslim Philosophers' Classifications of the Sciences', p. 81.
46 I have adopted here the translation of *ḥiyal* in its technical sense used by the *Encyclopaedia of Islam*: see Schacht, art. 'Ḥiyal', EI^2, vol. 3, p. 511.
47 Al-Fārābī, *Iḥṣā' al-ʿUlūm*, pp. 54–76 (Arabic), pp. 145–56 (Latin), pp. 39–53 (Spanish).
48 ibid., pp. 76, 83 (Arabic), pp. 157, 161 (Latin), pp. 55, 59–60 (Spanish).
49 Al-Rabe, 'Muslim Philosophers' Classifications of the Sciences', p. 93.
50 Al-Fārābī, *Iḥṣā' al-ʿUlūm*, pp. 83–7 (Arabic), pp. 161–3 (Latin), pp. 60–2 (Spanish).
51 ibid., pp. 87–9 (Arabic), pp. 163–5 (Latin), pp. 63–4 (Spanish).
52 See Fakhry, *A History of Islamic Philosophy*, p. 14.
53 Al-Fārābī, *Iḥṣā' al-ʿUlūm*, p. 89 (Arabic), pp. 164–5 (Latin), p. 64 (Spanish). For the negative vocabulary of al-Fārābī, see Netton, *Allāh Transcendent*, pp. 104–7.
54 Al-Rabe, 'Muslim Philosophers' Classifications of the Sciences', p. 81.
55 Al-Fārābī, *Kitāb al-Tanbīh*, p. 20.
56 ibid.
57 See above.
58 See al-Rabe, 'Muslim Philosophers' Classifications of the Sciences', p. 12.

59 Al-Fārābī, *Kitāb al-Tanbīh*, p. 19; al-Rabe, 'Muslim Philosophers' Classifications of the Sciences', pp. 12–13.
60 See above.
61 Jolivet, 'L'Intellect selon al-Fārābī: Quelques Remarques', *Bulletin d'Études Orientales*, vol. 29 (1977), p. 251.
62 Netton, *Allāh Transcendent*, pp. 116–17.
63 Jolivet, 'L'Intellect selon al-Fārābī', p. 251.
64 ibid., p. 256.
65 ibid., p. 251.
66 See ibid., p. 252.
67 Al-Fārābī, *Risāla fī 'l-ʿAql*, p. 3.
68 ibid., pp. 3–4.
69 ibid., pp. 4–7 (1st), 7–8 (2nd), 8–9 (3rd), 9–12 (4th), 35–6 (6th).
70 ibid., p. 4.
71 ibid., pp. 12–35.
72 ibid., p. 12.
73 ibid., pp. 3–4; see Jolivet, 'L'Intellect selon al-Fārābī', p. 252.
74 See al-Fārābī, *Risāla fī 'l-ʿAql*, p. 29; Davidson, 'Alfarabi and Avicenna on the Active Intellect', *Viator*, vol. 3 (1972), pp. 150–1; Netton, *Allāh Transcendent*, p. 118; see Plotinus, *Enneads*, V.1.2.
75 Al-Fārābī, *Kitāb al-Ḥurūf*, p. xi (English preface).
76 ibid.
77 Aristotle, *Metaphysics* Book Gamma, 1003^a21–1003^a33, trans. Kirwan, *Aristotle's Metaphysics: Books Γ, Δ and E*, p. 1.
78 Kirwan, *Aristotle's Metaphysics: Books Γ, Δ and E*, p. 76.
79 Al-Fārābī, *Kitāb al-Ḥurūf*, see pp. 41, 56 (Arabic introd.) and *passim*.
80 Al-Fārābī, *Kitāb al-Ḥurūf*, pp. 61, 131, 162.
81 See ibid., pp. 164ff.
82 ibid., pp. 66–9, xiii.
83 See above, p. 39.
84 See al-Fārābī, *Kitāb al-Ḥurūf*, p. 70.
85 See above, n. 55; see al-Fārābi, *Kitāb al-Ḥurūf*, p. 69.
86 Al-Fārābī, *Kitāb al-Ḥurūf*, pp. 165–81; see Arnaldez, 'Pensée et Langage', p. 59.
87 See al-Fārābī, *Kitāb al-Ḥurūf*, pp. 165–6; Arnaldez, 'Pensée et Langage', p. 59.
88 See al-Fārābī, *Kitāb al-Ḥurūf*, p. 171.
89 See Walzer, *Al-Farabi on the Perfect State*, pp. 70, 72 (Arabic text); Netton, *Allāh Transcendent*, p. 106; Arnaldez, 'Pensée et Langage', p. 57.
90 Al-Fārābī, *Risāla fī 'l-ʿAql*, pp. 3–7; Badawī, *Histoire de la Philosophie en Islam*, vol. 2, pp. 546–7; Fakhry, *A History of Islamic Philosophy*, p. 121; Liddell and Scott, *An Intermediate Greek-English Lexicon*, p. 872; Wehr, *Dictionary of Modern Written Arabic*, p. 630.
91 Al-Fārābī, *Risāla fī 'l-ʿAql*, pp. 3, 7–8; Badawī, *Histoire de la Philosophie en Islam*, vol. 2, pp. 546–7; Fakhry, *A History of Islamic Philosophy*, p. 121.
92 Al-Fārābī, *Risāla fī 'l-ʿAql*, pp. 3, 8–9; Badawī, *Histoire de la Philosophie en Islam*, vol. 2, pp. 546–7; Fakhry, *A History of Islamic Philosophy*, p. 121.
93 Al-Fārābī, *Risāla fī 'l-ʿAql*, pp. 4, 9–12; Badawī, *Histoire de la Philosophie en Islam*, vol. 2, pp. 546–7; Fakhry, *A History of Islamic Philosophy*, p. 121.
94 Al-Fārābī, *Risāla fī 'l-ʿAql*, pp. 4, 12–35; Badawī, *Histoire de la Philosophie en Islam*,

vol. 2, pp. 546, 548–54; Fakhry, *A History of Islamic Philosophy*, pp. 121–2.

95 Fakhry, *A History of Islamic Philosophy*, p. 121.

96 Trans. Arthur Hyman, 'Alfarabi: The Letter Concerning the Intellect', in Hyman and Walsh (eds), *Philosophy in the Middle Ages*, p. 215; see, for the original Arabic, al-Fārābī, *Risāla fī 'l-ʿAql*, pp. 12–14; see also Badawī, *Histoire de la Philosophie en Islam*, vol. 2, pp. 548–9; Fakhry, *A History of Islamic Philosophy*, p. 121.

97 Fakhry, *A History of Islamic Philosophy*, p. 121.

98 (My italics) trans. Hyman, 'Alfarabi: The Letter Concerning the Intellect', pp. 215–16. See, for the original Arabic, al-Fārābī, *Risāla fī 'l-ʿAql*, p. 15. See also Badawī, *Histoire de la Philosophie en Islam*, vol. 2, pp. 549–50.

99 Madkour, 'Al-Fārābī', p. 461.

100 Fakhry, *A History of Islamic Philosophy*, pp. 121–2.

101 Trans. Hyman, 'Alfarabi: The Letter Concerning the Intellect', p. 217. See, for the original Arabic, al-Fārābī, *Risāla fī 'l-ʿAql*, p. 20; see also Badawī, *Histoire de la Philosophie en Islam*, vol. 2, pp. 551–2; and Hyman and Walsh (eds), *Philosophy in the Middle Ages*, p. 213.

102 Badawī, *Histoire de la Philosophie en Islam*, vol. 2, p. 552.

103 Trans. Hyman, 'Alfarabi: The Letter Concerning the Intellect', p. 218. See, for the original Arabic, al-Fārābī, *Risāla fī 'l-ʿAql*, pp. 24–5; see also Badawī, *Histoire de la Philosophie en Islam*, vol. 2, pp. 552–4 and Fakhry, *A History of Islamic Philosophy*, p. 122.

104 See Netton, *Allāh Transcendent*, pp. 115–19.

105 See Walzer, 'Al-Fārābī's Theory of Prophecy and Divination' in Walzer, *Greek into Arabic*, p. 209.

106 Jolivet, 'L'Intellect selon al-Fārābī', p. 253.

107 ibid.

108 See Madkour, 'Al-Fārābī', p. 461; O'Leary, *Arabic Thought and its Place in History*, p. 148.

109 ibid.

110 O'Leary, *Arabic Thought and its Place in History*, pp. 148–9.

111 See Netton, *Allāh Transcendent*, p. 117 and Hyman and Walsh (eds), *Philosophy in the Middle Ages*, p. 213.

112 Walzer, 'Al-Fārābī's Theory of Prophecy and Divination', pp. 209–10.

113 See the longer quotations cited above from al-Fārābī's *Risāla fī 'l-ʿAql*.

114 See Fakhry, *A History of Islamic Philosophy*, pp. 122–3.

115 (My italics) trans. Hyman, 'Alfarabi: The Letter Concerning the Intellect', p. 221. See, for the original Arabic, al-Fārābī, *Risāla fī 'l-ʿAql*, pp. 35–6.

116 See Netton, *Allāh Transcendent*, esp. pp. 114–23.

117 ibid., p. 117.

118 See ibid., p. 116, Fig. 2.

119 See al-Fārābī, *Risāla fī 'l-ʿAql*, p. 36. This is also, confusingly, the case in one of our primary sources (cited in Figure 2) for the tenfold Neoplatonic register, *al-Madīna al-Fāḍila*: see Walzer, *Al-Farabi on the Perfect State*, pp. 80–1, where *God* is characterized as 'the First Cause, the First Intellect and the First Living' (*al-Sabab al-Awwal wa 'l-ʿAql al-Awwal wa 'l-Ḥayy al-Awwal*). Al-Fārābī's preferred designation here of the first actual *emanation* from God, i.e. the First Intellect, is 'the Second' (*al-Thānī*) (see Walzer, *Al-Farabi on the Perfect State*, pp. 100–1, Netton, *Allāh Transcendent*, pp. 115–16).

120 Badawī, *Histoire de la Philosophie en Islam*, vol. 2, p. 545.
121 Fakhry, *A History of Islamic Philosophy*, p. 123.
122 ibid., p. 127.

3 The Epistemological Substrate of Fārābism (ii): In the Steps of Their Master

1 For an English translation, see Rescher and Shehadi, 'Yaḥyā ibn ʿAdī's Treatise "On the Four Scientific Questions Regarding the Art of Logic"', *Journal of the History of Ideas*, vol. XXV (Oct.–Dec. 1964), pp. 572–8; for the Arabic text, see Mubahat Türker (ed.), 'Yaḥyā Ibn ʿ Adī ve Neşredilmemiş bir Risalesi', *Ankara Üniversitesi Dil ve Tarih-Coğrafya Fakültesi Dergisi*, vol. XIV, nos 1–2 (1956), pp. 87–102. (This also contains a Turkish translation.). See also Endress, *The Works of Yaḥyā ibn ʿAdī*, pp. 42–3.
2 Rosenthal, *Knowledge Triumphant*, p. 209.
3 ibid., p. 208.
4 (My italics) trans. Dunlop, 'Al-Fārābī's Introductory *Risālah* on Logic', *Islamic Quarterly*, vol. 3 (1956), pp. 230, 232. The original Arabic text will be found on pp. 225, 227.
5 My italics.
6 Rescher and Shehadi, 'Yaḥyā ibn Adī's Treatise "On the Four Scientific Questions"', pp. 573–4; for the Arabic text, see Türker (ed.), 'Yaḥyā Ibn ʿAdī', p. 98.
7 See Rescher and Shehadi, 'Yaḥyā ibn ʿAdī's Treatise "On the Four Scientific Questions"', p. 573.
8 ibid., p. 574; for the Arabic text see Türker (ed.) 'Yaḥyā Ibn ʿAdī', p. 98.
9 Rescher and Shehadi, 'Yaḥyā ibn ʿAdī's Treatise "On the Four Scientific Questions"', p. 575; for the Arabic text see Türker (ed.) 'Yaḥyā Ibn ʿAdī', p. 99.
10 ibid.
11 Rescher and Shehadi, 'Yaḥyā ibn ʿAdī's Treatise "On the Four Scientific Questions"', p. 576; for the Arabic text see Türker (ed.), 'Yaḥyā Ibn ʿAdī', p. 100.
12 Rescher and Shehadi, 'Yaḥyā ibn ʿAdī's Treatise "On the Four Scientific Questions"', pp. 576–7; for the Arabic text see Türker (ed.), 'Yaḥyā Ibn ʿAdī', p. 101.
13 See al-Takriti, *Yahya Ibn ʿAdi*, pp. 11–12; Samir, 'Le Tahḏīb al-Aḫlāq', esp. pp. 137–8.
14 Al-Takriti, *Yahya Ibn ʿAdi*, p. 256.
15 ibid., p. 222.
16 (My italics) Walzer, art. 'Akhlāḳ', *EI*², vol. 1, p. 328.
17 Al-Takriti, *Yahya Ibn ʿAdi*, p. 230; for the Arabic text see p. 67.
18 Al-Takriti, *Yahya Ibn ʿAdi*, p. 67 (Arabic text), p. 161 (English summary of *Tahdhīb al-Akhlāq*).
19 ibid., p. 71 (Arabic text), p. 162 (English summary). I am, of course, well aware of the profound objections by modern animal lovers to those types of phrase which seek to denigrate animals at the expense of human beings. One can only point out here that the denigratory phrases are Yaḥyā's, and that he was writing in an age where any concept of animals' rights would have been ignored. There were, of course, exceptions: for a brief survey of the kindliness of the Prophet Muḥammad towards animals, see Guillaume, *Traditions of Islam*, pp. 106–7; see

also, by contrast, the verdict of the *Shāh* at the 'Debate of the Animals' in the *Rasā'il* of the Ikhwān al-Ṣafā' (Netton, *Muslim Neoplatonists*, p. 92; *Rasā'il*, vol. 2, p. 377).

20 Al-Takriti, *Yahya Ibn ʿAdi*, p. 72 (Arabic text), p. 162 (English summary).

21 ibid., p. 162 (English summary).

22 ibid., p. 72 (Arabic text), p. 162 (English summary).

23 ibid., pp. 121, 142 (Arabic text), pp. 172, 174 (English summary).

24 Matthew 5: 48 (trans. Knox).

25 See above, n. 9.

26 Al-Takriti, *Yahya Ibn ʿAdi*, p. 79 (Arabic text), 163–4 (English summary). For the general background to Figure 3, see Plato, *The Republic*, Bk IV: 435–44 (Penguin edn, trans. Lee: pp. 183–98). See also Fakhry, *A History of Islamic Philosophy*, p. 193 and al-Takriti, *Yahya Ibn ʿAdi*, p. 73 (Arabic text), p. 162 (English summary), 224–6. The translation of the Arabic Platonic terms is by no means uniform: those used in Figure 3 are Fakhry's translations. Al-Takriti's renditions are 'appetitive', 'courageous' and 'rational', while Walzer, discussing Miskawaih, uses 'appetitive', 'spirited' and 'rational' ('Some Aspects …', p. 221). Lee, translating from the Platonic Greek, gives 'desire' or 'irrational appetite'; 'anger', 'indignation' or 'spirit'; and 'reason'. (Plato, as Lee points out (ibid., p. 185) 'in any case never developed a precise terminology'.) Hare uses the terms 'desire', 'spirit' and 'reason' (Hare, *Plato*, p. 53) to render the original Greek.

In the discussion of Platonic and Islamic intellection, the non-specialist reader should not be confused by the term 'soul' (Arabic *nafs*, Greek *psukhé*). It frequently had a sense rather different from the contemporary one, or rather several senses. Thus we find modern authors writing about Plato using the words 'soul' and 'mind' interchangeably. An example is R.M. Hare, whose short volume *Plato*, is, however, a brilliant model of lucidity. For example, Hare notes that '[The early Pythagoreans] thought, as Plato was to think, that the soul or mind (*psȳchē*) was an entity distinct and separable from the body. This was consonant with primitive Greek thinking about the soul' (p. 11). Again, he writes: 'And along with investigations about the status of the things known, Plato had to face problems about the person who is doing the knowing and about his relation to these things. His account of the soul or mind was to become the framework which held together his entire philosophy. The division of the mind into 'faculties' or 'powers' or even 'parts' enabled him to assign different kinds of mental activity to these different parts and thus, he thought, distinguish them more clearly' (pp. 19–20). The Greek *psukhé* (or, to use Hare's transliteration, *psȳchē*) means 'the soul', 'mind', 'understanding', 'breath', 'spirit' and 'ghost' among a variety of meanings listed in Liddell and Scott, *An Intermediate Greek-English Lexicon*, p. 903.

I am much indebted to my colleague, Dr Christopher Gill, Senior Lecturer in Classics at the University of Exeter, for providing me with the following very full written comment in response to a query of mine about Plato's use of vocabulary: 'In the *Republic*, Plato's typical term for the rational part of the *psukhé* is *logistikón*, i.e. the part of the soul which has reason (*logos*) and can make the soul as a whole live according to reason. N.B. This is a *part* of the *psukhé*; Plato does not talk about "the rational soul" or use *psukhé* on its own to signify *to logistikón*. Plato does also use *nous* and cognates, for example, in analysing degrees of knowledge or understanding in Book 6 of the *Republic*. But Plato uses *to logis-*

tikón and cognates in this work as his "standard" term for the rational part of the soul; see, for example, 441E and 442C in Book 4. He does so, I think, because he wants to present reason not just as "intellectual" (capable of thought) but as the agent of practical as well as theoretical activity, i.e. the element capable of "taking care of the *psukhé* as a whole" (441E), as well as that which enables philosopher kings to take care of the state as a whole. But Plato is studiously non-technical in his vocabulary and emphasizes different aspects of rationality at different times. For example, in Book 9 of the *Republic*, in the version of the tripartite *psukhé* he gives there, he stresses the knowledge-*loving* aspect of reason (581B).' Dr Gill's comments should be borne in mind when analysing the development and extension of Platonic vocabulary at the hands not only of the School of Fārābī, which is the subject of this book, but of any of those Islamic philosophers who might have absorbed in one degree or another the vocabulary and doctrines of Plato.

27 Al-Takriti, *Yahya Ibn ʿAdi*, p. 79 (Arabic text), pp. 163–4 (English summary).
28 ibid., p. 230 (English summary).
29 ibid., p. 231 (English summary).
30 See ibid., pp. 79–82 (Arabic text), pp. 163–4 (English summary).
31 ibid., pp. 117–18 (Arabic text), pp. 171–2 (English summary).
32 ibid., p. 199 (The Background); see also pp. 200–2.
33 ibid.
34 See above, n. 16.
35 Al-Takriti, *Yahya Ibn ʿAdi*, p. 199 (The Background).
36 See above, n. 16.
37 Al-Takriti, *Yahya Ibn ʿAdi*, pp. 208–9 (The Background). See also pp. 210–21.
38 ibid., p. 210.
39 See chapter 1, n. 57 for full references.
40 Fakhry, *A History of Islamic Philosophy*, p. 198 (n. 54).
41 ibid., p. 201.
42 Yaḥyā b. ʿAdī, *Maqāla fī ʾl-Tawḥīd*, ed. Samir.
43 Endress, *The Works of Yaḥyā ibn ʿAdī*, pp. 72–3.
44 ibid., p. 73.
45 ibid.; see Yaḥyā b. ʿAdī, *Maqāla fī ʾl-Tawḥīd*, ed. Samir, pp. 242–64.
46 Endress, *The Works of Yaḥyā ibn ʿAdī*, p. 73.
47 Yaḥyā b. ʿAdī, *Maqāla fī ʾl-Tawḥīd*, ed. Samir, p. xix.
48 ibid.
49 (My italics); Endress, *The Works of Yaḥyā ibn ʿAdī*, p. 73.
50 See Yaḥyā b. ʿAdī, *Maqāla fī ʾl-Tawḥīd*, ed. Samir p. xix.
51 ibid. See also Endress, *The Works of Yaḥyā ibn ʿAdī*, p. 73; Proclus, *The Elements of Theology* (ed. Dodds), esp. pp. 106–7 (Prop. 121), 264. See also Rowson, *A Muslim Philosopher on the Soul and its Fate: Al-ʿĀmirī's* Kitāb al-Amad ʿalā l-Abad, p. 227.
52 Yaḥyā b. ʿAdī, *Maqāla fī ʾl-Tawḥīd*, ed. Samir, p. xx; see Netton, *Allāh Transcendent*, pp. 224, 106, 155.
53 Netton, *Allāh Transcendent*, p. 224.
54 Kraemer, *Humanism in the Renaissance of Islam*, p. 107.
55 For example, see Walzer, *Al-Farabi on the Perfect State*, pp. 245–9.
56 Fakhry, *A History of Islamic Philosophy*, pp. 182–3.
57 Review of Kraemer, *Philosophy in the Renaissance of Islam*, in *Journal of the Royal Asiatic Society*, no. 1 (1988), p. 174.

58 Kraemer, 'Abû Sulaymân As-Sijistânî' (Ph.D. thesis), p. 45. However, by way of contrast, see al-Qāḍī, '*Kitāb Ṣiwān al-Ḥikma*: Structure, Composition, Authorship and Sources', *Der Islam*, vol. 58 (1981), esp. pp. 117–19, where al-Qāḍī suggests that the real author of the *Ṣiwān* is one 'Abū al-Qāsim al-Kātib, known as Ghulām al-ʿĀmirī'. He elaborates: 'As his name indicates, Abū al-Qāsim was the disciple of Abū al-Ḥasan al-ʿĀmirī, possibly at an early stage in his life his slave too. He studied philosophy with al-ʿĀmirī and used to teach al-ʿĀmirī's books to students.' While noting here the interesting remarks of al-Qāḍī, this book follows Badawī, Dunlop, Kraemer and Stern in attributing the *Ṣiwān al-Ḥikma* to al-Sijistānī. Gutas also shares this attribution (see his *Greek Wisdom Literature*).

59 Al-Sijistānī, Muntakhab, ed. Dunlop, p. xxiii (English introd.).

60 Fakhry, *A History of Islamic Philosophy*, p. 182.

61 See the very useful and comprehensive survey of the contents of the *Ṣiwān* in al-Sijistānī, *Muntakhab*, ed. Dunlop, pp. xxxiii–xxxvii (English introd.).

62 Kraemer, *Philosophy in the Renaissance of Islam*, p. 268 translating al-Tawḥīdī, *al-Muqābasāt*, p. 283. See also al-Takriti, *Yahya Ibn ʿAdi*, p. 258 (Contribution to Ethical Thought), and Kraemer, 'Abû Sulaymân As-Sijistânî' (Ph.D. thesis), p. 49.

63 Kraemer, 'Abû Sulaymân As-Sijistânî' (Ph.D. thesis), p. 249 referring to al-Tawḥīdī, *al-Imtāʿ*, pt. 3, p. 119.

64 Al-Tawḥīdī, *al-Imtāʿ*, pt. 3, p. 110; see al-Sijistānī, *Muntakhab* ed. Badawī, pp. 25–6 (French introd.).

65 Kraemer, 'Abû Sulaymân As-Sijistânî' (Ph.D thesis), p. 245 citing al-Tawḥīdī, *al-Imtāʿ*, pt. 3, p. 108.

66 Kraemer, 'Abû Sulaymân As-Sijistânî' (Ph.D thesis), p. 415 (n. 371).

67 Kraemer, *Philosophy in the Renaissance of Islam*, p. 226 referring to al-Tawḥīdī, *al-Imtāʿ*, pt. 3, pp. 108–10.

68 See Kraemer, *Philosophy in the Renaissance of Islam*, p. 227.

69 Kraemer, 'Abû Sulaymân As-Sijistânî' (Ph.D. thesis), p. 248.

70 Kraemer, *Philosophy in the Renaissance of Islam*, p. 227.

71 Kraemer, 'Abû Sulaymân As-Sijistânî' (Ph.D. thesis), p. 250.

72 ibid., p. 249.

73 Kraemer, *Philosophy in the Renaissance of Islam*, pp. 258–9 referring to al-Tawḥīdī, *al-Muqābasāt*, p. 320.

74 Kraemer, 'Abû Sulaymân As-Sijistânî' (Ph.D. thesis), p. 250.

75 Kraemer, *Philosophy in the Renaissance of Islam*, p. 261 referring to al-Tawḥīdī, *al-Muqābasāt*, pp. 318–19.

76 See Kraemer, *Philosophy in the Renaissance of Islam*, p. 260.

77 Al-Sijistānī, *Muntakhab*, ed. Badawī, p. 24 (French introd.).

78 ibid.; al-Tawḥīdī, *al-Imtāʿ*, pt. 3, p. 116.

79 Stern, art. 'Abū Sulaymān . . .', p. 151.

80 Kraemer, 'Abû Sulaymân As-Sijistânî' (Ph.D. thesis), p. 202 referring to al-Tawḥīdī, *al-Imtāʿ*, pt. 3, p. 119.

81 Trans. Kraemer from 'On the Specific Perfection of the Human Species' in *Philosophy in the Renaissance of Islam*, p. 299. The original Arabic of this text, *Fī 'l-Kamāl al-Khāṣṣ bi-Nawʿ al-Insān*, will be found at the back of al-Sijistānī, *Muntakhab*, ed. Badawī, pp. 381–2.

82 Kraemer, *Philosophy in the Renaissance of Islam*, p. 276.

83 See *Fī 'l-Kamāl al-Khāṣṣ bi-Nawʿ al-Insān*, in al-Sijistānī, *Muntakhab*, ed. Badawī, pp. 378–9. See also Kraemer, *Philosophy in the Renaissance of Islam*, pp. 276, 294.
84 Al-Tawḥīdī, *al-Imtaʿ*, pt. 2, p. 45.
85 Trans. Rosenthal, *Knowledge Triumphant*, p. 319, from al-Sijistānī, *Muntakhab*, ed. Dunlop, p. 85 (Arabic text).
86 (My italics) trans. Rosenthal, *Knowledge Triumphant*, pp. 326–7 from al-Tawḥīdī, *al-Imtāʿ*, pt. 2, p. 49.
87 Al-Tawḥīdī, *al-Muqābasāt*, p. 249.
88 See Kraemer, *Philosophy in the Renaissance of Islam*, p. 263 (n. 285).
89 Al-Tawḥīdī, *al Muqābasāt*, p. 269.
90 ibid.
91 See notes to chapter 2, n. 8.
92 Kraemer, *Philosophy in the Renaissance of Islam*, p. 263.
93 Jadaane, 'La Philosophie de Sijistānī', *Studia Islamica*, vol. XXXIII (1971), p. 81.
94 ibid.
95 Al-Tawḥīdī, *al-Imtāʿ*, pt. 1, p. 40.
96 ibid.
97 Jadaane, 'La Philosophie de Sijistānī', p. 84.
98 Al-Tawḥīdī, *al-Muqābasāt*, p. 139 (see esp. n. 2); Jadaane, 'La Philosophie de Sijistānī', p. 81.
99 Jadaane, 'La Philosophie de Sijistānī', p. 82 reads '*monde*/world' (=*al-ʿālam*) rather than 'knowledge' (*ʿilm*).
100 Al-Tawḥīdī, *al-Muqābasāt*, p. 139; Jadaane, 'La Philosophie de Sijistānī', pp. 81–2.
101 Al-Tawḥīdī, *al-Muqābasāt*, p. 139; Jadaane, 'La Philosophie de Sijistānī', p. 82.
102 Jadaane, 'La Philosophie de Sijistānī', p. 82. For more on this latter category, see ibid., pp. 82–3.
103 See ibid., p. 80.
104 See above, n. 87.
105 See al-Tawḥīdī, *al-Imtāʿ*, pt. 2, p. 83.
106 ibid.
107 See above, n. 98.
108 Kraemer, 'Abû Sulaymân As-Sijistânî' (Ph.D. thesis), p. 266.
109 Al-Takriti, *Yahya Ibn ʿAdi*, p. 257 (Contribution to Ethical Thought).
110 ibid., p. 259.
111 Kraemer, *Philosophy in the Renaissance of Islam*, pp. 268–9.
112 Al-Tawḥīdī, *al-Imtāʿ*, pt. 3, p. 130, cited and trans. in Kraemer, *Philosophy in the Renaissance of Islam*, p. 269.
113 See Kraemer, *Philosophy in the Renaissance of Islam*, p. 269.
114 Rowson, *A Muslim Philosopher on the Soul and its Fate: Al-ʿĀmirī's* Kitāb al-Amad ʿalā l-Abad (hereafter abbreviated to *Kitāb al-Amad*), p. v.
115 ibid., pp. 3, 21, 29.
116 Al-ʿĀmirī, *Kitāb al-Saʿāda wa 'l-Isʿād.*
117 Al-ʿĀmirī, *Kitāb al-Amad*, pp. 16–17.
118 Vadet, *Une Défense Philosophique de la Sunna*, p. 16.
119 Rowson, art, 'Al-ʿĀmirī', *EI² Supp.*, Fascs 1–2, p. 72.
120 Allard, 'Un Philosophe Théologien: Muḥammad b. Yūsuf al-ʿĀmirī', *Revue de l'Histoire des Religions*, vol. 187 (1975), p. 59.
121 Al-ʿĀmirī, *Kitāb al-Amad*, pp. 56–9, 182–5.

122 Al-ʿĀmirī, *Kitāb al-Iʿlām bi Manāqib al-Islām* (hereafter abbreviated to *Kitāb al-Iʿlām*).
123 Al-ʿĀmirī, *Kitāb al-Amad*, p. 21; see also Rowson, art. 'Al-ʿĀmirī', p. 72.
124 Al-ʿĀmirī, *Kitāb al-Amad*, pp. 56, 58 (Arabic text), pp. 57, 59 (trans.).
125 Al-ʿĀmirī, *Kitāb al-Iʿlām*, p. 84.
126 Al-ʿĀmirī, *Kitāb al-Saʿāda*, p. 58.
127 Al-ʿĀmirī, p. 76 (Arabic text), p. 77 (trans.).
128 (My italics) al-ʿĀmirī, *Kitāb al-Iʿlām*, p. 78.
129 Trans. Rowson in *Kitāb al-Amad*, p. 101; for the Arabic see p. 100.
130 Al-ʿĀmirī, *Kitāb al-Amad*, p. 56 (Arabic text), p. 57 (trans.).
131 ibid.
132 Al-ʿĀmirī, *Kitāb al-Iʿlām*, pp. 84–5; see also Rosenthal, *Classical Heritage in Islam*, p. 63 and al-ʿĀmirī, *Kitāb al-Amad*, p. 189.
133 See al-ʿĀmirī, *Kitāb al-Iʿlām*, pp. 88ff.; Rosenthal, *Classical Heritage*, pp. 65ff.
134 Trans. Rosenthal, *Classical Heritage*, p. 69 from al-ʿÂmirī, *Kitāb al-Iʿlām*, p. 95.
135 Arkoun, 'Logocentrisme et Vérité Religieuse dans la Pensée Islamique d'après *al-Iʿlām bi-Manāqib al-Islām* d'al-ʿÂmirī', *Studia Islamica*, vol. XXXV (1972), pp. 5–51.
136 ibid., p. 18.
137 See ibid., p. 19.
138 Al-ʿĀmirī, *Kitāb al-Amad*, pp. 8, 20.
139 ibid.
140 See ibid., pp. 20, 22.
141 ibid., p. 22.
142 ibid.
143 (My italics) al-ʿĀmirī, *Kitāb al-Amad*, p. 94 (Arabic text), p. 95 (trans.).
144 ibid., p. 108 (Arabic text), p. 109 (trans.).
145 ibid., p. 96 (Arabic text), p. 97 (trans.).
146 ibid., p. 249 (Commentary).
147 See ibid., esp. p. 84 (Arabic text), p. 85 (trans.).
148 ibid., p. 264 (Commentary). Note the very useful diagram provided by Rowson. See also ibid., p. 90 (Arabic text), p. 91 (trans.); p. 114 (Arabic text), p. 115 (trans.).
149 See Kraemer, *Humanism in the Renaissance of Islam*, pp. 212, 222, 233.
150 ibid., p. 213.
151 See ibid.; see also Stern, art. 'Abū Ḥayyān al-Tawḥīdī', p. 127.
152 See Stern, art. 'Abū Ḥayyān al-Tawḥīdī', p. 127; see also Netton, *Muslim Neoplatonists*, p. 3.
153 Hamdani, 'Abū Ḥayyān al-Tawḥīdī and the Brethren of Purity', *International Journal of Middle East Studies*, vol. 9 (1978), p. 345.
154 See ibid., *passim*.
155 ibid., pp. 348–9.
156 Ikhwān al-Ṣafā', *Rasā'il*, vol. 2, pp. 178–378.
157 However, L.E. Goodman notes (*The Case of the Animals versus Man*, pp. 1–3):

> The knowledge which the Ikhwân do possess regarding the animal world is closer to love than to science ... [Moreover] the taxonomy presented by the Ikhwân, although crude and in some places apparently contrived ... is not a changing system. Rather its lines are fixed. The

animals belong to kinds (*ajnâs*), and these frequently are spoken of in familial terms ... the fixity of species and of kinds is regarded as a necessary consequence of the dependence of all natural things on a timeless and therefore changeless cause in the 'intellectual realm' of the World Soul. As in the scheme of Aristotle, fluidity and change extend only to particulars as such. But, unlike orthodox Aristotelians, the Ikhwân al-Ṣafâ' are not bound strictly by the notion of fixity of nature in its accustomed course.

158 Al-Tawḥīdī, *Kitāb Al-Imtā'*, pt. 1, pp. 159–96; see Kopf, 'The Zoological Chapter of the *Kitāb al-Imtā' wal-Mu'ānasa* of Abū Ḥayyān al-Tauḥīdī (10th Century)', *Osiris*, vol. XII (1956), pp. 390–466, which provides an introduction, annotated translation, emendations of the Arabic text used, and index.
159 Kopf, 'The Zoological Chapter', p. 397.
160 See ibid.
161 ibid., p. 399.
162 Kraemer, *Humanism in the Renaissance of Islam*, p. 220.
163 Stern, art. 'Abū Ḥayyān al-Tawḥīdī', p. 127.
164 See ibid.; see also Kraemer, *Humanism in the Renaissance of Islam*, p. 222.
165 See Kraemer, *Humanism in the Renaissance of Islam*, p. 219; Kraemer, *Philosophy in the Renaissance of Islam*, p. 31.
166 See Kopf, 'The Zoological Chapter', p. 392.
167 Rosenthal, 'Abū Ḥayyān at-Tawḥīdī on Penmanship', in Rosenthal, *Four Essays on Art and Literature in Islam*, p. 20.
168 For a critical edition, with a French introduction and translation, together with a glossary of technical terms, see Marc Bergé, 'Épitre sur les Sciences (*Risāla fī 'l-'Ulūm*) d'Abū Ḥayyān at-Tawḥīdī (310/922(?)–414/1023): Introduction, Traduction, Glossaire Technique, Manuscrit et Édition Critique', *Bulletin d'Études Orientales* (Institut Français de Damas), vol. XVIII (1963–4), pp. 241–300. The Arabic text is to be found on pp. 286–98. (This whole work is hereafter referred to as Bergé, *Risāla fī 'l-'Ulūm*). See also Bergé's supplementary to the above: 'Épitre sur les Sciences (*Risāla fī 'l-'Ulūm*) d'Abū Ḥayyān al-Tawḥīdī (310/922(?)–414/1023): Glossaire et Index Analytique', *Bulletin d'Études Orientales*, vol. XXI (1968), pp. 313–46.
169 Al-Tawḥīdī, *Al-Muqābasāt*, p. 362.
170 ibid.
171 Trans. Rosenthal, *Knowledge Triumphant*, p. 249 from al-Tawḥīdī, *al-Baṣā'ir*, vol. 1, p. 389. Rosenthal cites al-Tawḥīdī referring to a poet for whom knowledge 'restores people and quenches their thirst, like as rain falling upon wood gives it new life' (*Knowledge Triumphant*, p. 320).
172 Trans. Rosenthal, 'Abū Ḥayyān at-Tawḥīdī on Penmanship', p. 39; for the Arabic text see *Risāla fī 'Ilm al-Kitāba*, p. 41 in al-Tawḥīdī, *Thalāth Rasā'il.*
173 Trans. Rosenthal, 'Abū Ḥayyān at-Tawḥīdī on Penmanship', p. 38; al-Tawḥīdī, *Risāla fī 'Ilm al-Kitāba*, p. 40.
174 Trans. Rosenthal, 'Abū Ḥayyān at-Tawḥīdī on Penmanship', p. 41; al-Tawḥīdī, *Risāla fī 'Ilm al-Kitāba*, p. 42.
175 Trans. Rosenthal, 'Abū Ḥayyān at-Tawḥīdī on Penmanship', p. 38; al-Tawḥīdī, *Risāla fī 'Ilm al-Kitāba*, p. 40.
176 ibid.

177 Al-Tawḥīdī, *al-Imtāʿ*, pt. 1, p. 147.
178 See Bergé, *Pour un Humanisme Vécu*, p. 284.
179 See Rosenthal, *Knowledge Triumphant*, p. 241.
180 Al-Tawḥīdī, *al-Baṣāʾir*, vol. I, p. 299.
181 Rosenthal, *Knowledge Triumphant*, p. 316.
182 Al-Tawḥīdī, *al-Imtāʿ*, pt. 2, p. 10.
183 See Bergé, *Pour un Humanisme Vécu*, p. 289.
184 Bergé, *Risāla fī 'l-ʿUlūm*, p. 243 (French introd.).
185 ibid., p. 297 (Arabic text), p. 257 (French trans.).
186 See ibid., pp. 246–8 (French introd.), pp. 286–98 (Arabic text), pp. 255–73 (French trans.).
187 ibid., p. 296 (Arabic text), p. 258 (French trans.).
188 ibid., p. 253 (French introd.).
189 ibid., p. 254 (French introd.).
190 See ibid.
191 ibid.
192 ibid., pp. 296–8 (Arabic text), pp. 255–7 (French trans.).
193 ibid., pp. 294–5 (Arabic text), pp. 258–61 (French trans.).
194 ibid., p. 291 (Arabic text), pp. 265–6 (French trans.).
195 See ibid., p. 287 (Arabic text), p. 272 (French trans.).
196 Kraemer, *Humanism in the Renaissance of Islam*, p. 222.
197 Al-Tawḥīdī, *al-Imtāʿ*, pt. 2, p. 34; see Rosenthal, *Knowledge Triumphant*, p. 319.
198 Rosenthal, *Knowledge Triumphant*, p. 247, citing Ibn al-Maṭrān, *Bustān al-Aṭibbāʾ* (ms. Army Medical Library).
199 Al-Tawḥīdī, *al-Baṣāʾir*, vol. 1, p. 7.
200 ibid., p. 8.
201 ibid.
202 See above, nn. 172ff.
203 Trans. Rosenthal, 'Abū Ḥayyān at-Tawḥīdī on Penmanship', p. 34; al-Tawḥīdī, *Risāla fī ʿIlm al-Kitāba*, p. 38.
204 Fakhry, *A History of Islamic Philosophy*, p. 183.
205 Kopf, 'The Zoological Chapter', p. 395.
206 ibid.
207 ibid., p. 396.
208 See ibid.

4 Conclusion

1 Hare, *Plato*, pp. 30, 31, 32.
2 ibid., p. 41.
3 ibid., p. 44.
4 ibid., p. 45.
5 ibid.
6 See ibid., p. 37.
7 Ibid., p. 45.
8 See Barnes, *Aristotle*, p. 22; Allan, *The Philosophy of Aristotle*, p. 117.
9 Barnes, *Aristotle*, p. 22.
10 See ibid., pp. 23–7.

11 ibid., p. 27.
12 Allan, *The Philosophy of Aristotle*, p. 123.
13 Aristotle, *The Politics* (ed. Everson), pp. xiii–xiv, see also p. xii.
14 Flew (ed.), *A Dictionary of Philosophy*, p. 101.
15 ibid., p. 102.
16 ibid.
17 ibid., pp. 198, 341.
18 Sorell, 'The Analysis of Knowledge', in Parkinson (ed.), *An Encyclopaedia of Philosophy*, pp. 128, 127. For a valuable survey of contemporary epistemology, see Dancy, *An Introduction to Contemporary Epistemology, passim.*
19 Sorell, 'The Analysis of Knowledge', p. 128.
20 ibid., p. 135.
21 For a fuller understanding of this Greek word, see Barnes, *Aristotle*, pp. 78–9.
22 To start, the reader is advised to consult the Bibliographical Guide (next chapter).
23 De Boer, *The History of Philosophy in Islam*, p. 126.
24 ibid., p. 128.

BIBLIOGRAPHY

Arabic Sources

(In this section 'al-' has been omitted from proper names at the beginning of an entry. Translations of texts are also included here.)

ʿĀmirī, Abū 'l-Ḥasan, *Kitāb al-Amad ʿalā 'l-Abad*, see Rowson (1988), *A Muslim Philosopher on the Soul and its Fate.*

—— *Kitāb al-Iʿlām bi-Manāqib al-Islām*, ed. A. Ghurāb, Cairo: Dār al-Kātib al-ʿArabī li 'l-Ṭibāʿa wa 'l-Nashr (1967).

—— *Kitāb al-Saʿāda wa 'l-Isʿād*, ed. M. Minovi, University of Tehran Publications, 435 (The Mahdavi Fund Series, 5), Wiesbaden: Franz Steiner Verlag (1957–8).

—— See also Rowson, 'Al-ʿĀmirī on the Afterlife'.

Arberry, A. J., *Poems of al-Mutanabbī* (Arabic-English text), Cambridge: Cambridge University Press (1967).

Badawī, ʿAbd al-Raḥmān (ed.), *Manṭiq Arisṭū*, pt. 3, Dirāsāt Islāmiyya, 7, Cairo: Maktabat al-Nahḍa al-Miṣriyya/Maṭbaʿa Dār al-Kutub al-Miṣriyya (1952).

—— See also Sijistānī and under Other Sources.

Bayhaqī, *Tārīkh Ḥukamā' al-Islām*, ed. Muḥammad Kurd ʿAlī, Damascus: al-Majmaʿ al-ʿIlmī al-ʿArabī (1946).

Bergé, Marc, 'Épitre sur les Sciences (*Risāla fī 'l-ʿUlūm*) d'Abū Ḥayyān at-Tawḥīdī (310/922(?)–414/1023): Introduction, Traduction, Glossaire Technique, Manuscrit et Édition Critique', *Bulletin d'Études Orientales* (Institut Français de Damas), vol. XVIII (1963–4), pp. 241–300 (Referred to in the notes as Bergé, *Risāla fī 'l-ʿUlūm*).

—— 'Épitre sur les Sciences (*Risāla fī 'l-ʿUlūm*) d'Abū Ḥayyān al-Tawḥīdī (310/922(?)–414/1023): Glossaire et Index Analytique', *Bulletin d'Études Orientales*, vol. XXI (1968), pp. 313–46.

Bosworth, C.E., *The History of al-Ṭabarī: Volume XXX. The ʿAbbāsid Caliphate in Equilibrium*, trans. and annot. by C.E. Bosworth, SUNY Series in Near Eastern Studies, Bibliotheca Persica, Albany, New York: State University of New York Press (1989).

Bouyges, Maurice, see Fārābī.

Dunlop, D.M., 'Al-Fārābī's Introductory *Risālah* on Logic', *Islamic Quarterly*, vol. 3

(1956), pp. 224–35. (Contains Arabic text pp. 225–30 and English trans. pp. 230–5.)

—— See also Fārābī, Sijistānī.

Fārābī, *Fuṣūl al-Madanī: Aphorisms of the Statesman*, ed. D.M. Dunlop, University of Cambridge Oriental Publications, 5, Cambridge: Cambridge University Press (1961).

—— *Iḥṣā' al-ʿUlūm (Catálogo de las Ciencias)*, 2nd edn, Arabic text ed. and trans. into Spanish by Angel Gonzalez Palencia (together with Gundissalinus' medieval Latin text), Madrid: Imprenta y Editorial Maestre (1953).

—— *Kitāb al-Ḥurūf*, Arabic text ed. with introd. and notes by Muhsin Mahdi, Rech. de l'Institut de Lettres Orientales de Beyrouth, Sér. I, tome XLVI, Beirut: Dār al-Mashriq (1969).

—— *Kitāb al-Mūsīqā al-Kabīr*, ed. Ghaṭṭās ʿAbd al-Malik Khashaba and Maḥmūd Aḥmad al-Ḥafnī, Turāthunā, Cairo: Dār al-Kātib al-ʿArabī li 'l-Ṭibāʿa wa 'l-Nashr (1967).

—— *Kitāb al-Siyāsa al-Madaniyya*, ed. Fauzi M. Najjar, Beirut: Imprimerie Catholique (1964).

—— *Kitāb al-Tanbīh ʿalā Sabīl al-Saʿāda*, Hyderabad: Dā'irat al-Maʿārif al-ʿUthmāniyya (1927).

—— *Risāla fī 'l-ʿAql*, texte Arabe intégral en partie inédit établi par Maurice Bouyges, Bibliotheca Arabica Scholasticorum, sér. Arabe, tome VIII, fasc. 1, Beirut: Imprimerie Catholique (1938).

—— See also Dunlop, Hyman, Walzer, Zimmermann.

Gibb, H.A.R., *The Travels of Ibn Baṭṭūṭa A.D. 1325–1354*, vol. 3, trans. by H.A.R. Gibb, Cambridge: Cambridge University Press for the Hakluyt Society (1971).

Gohlman, William E., *The Life of Ibn Sina: A Critical Edition and Annotated Translation*, Studies in Islamic Philosophy and Science, Albany, New York: State University of New York Press (1974).

Goodman, Lenn Evan, *The Case of the Animals versus Man Before the King of the Jinn: A Tenth-century Ecological Fable of the Pure Brethren of Basra*, Library of Classical Arabic Literature, III, Boston: Twayne Publishers (1978).

Gundissalinus, see Fārābī, *Iḥṣā' al-ʿUlūm*.

Hyman, Arthur (trans.), 'Alfarabi: The Letter Concerning the Intellect' in Hyman and Walsh (eds), *Philosophy in the Middle Ages*, Indianapolis: Hackett Publishing Co. (1987).

Ibn Abī Uṣaybiʿa, *Kitāb ʿUyūn al-Anbā' fī Ṭabaqāt al-Aṭibbā'*, Beirut: Dār Maktabat al-Ḥayāt (1965).

Ibn al-Qifṭī, *Tārīkh al-Ḥukamā'*, ed. J. Lippert, Leipzig: Dieterich'sche Verlagsbuchhandlung (Theodor Weicher) (1903).

Ibn Baṭṭūṭa, *Riḥla*, Beirut: Dār Ṣādir (1964).

—— See also Gibb.

Ibn Khallikān, *Wafayāt al-Aʿyān*, 8 vols, ed. Iḥsān ʿAbbās, Beirut: Dār al-Thaqāfa (1968–72).

Ibn Ṣāʿid (Ṣāʿid b. Aḥmad b. Ṣāʿid, al-Andalusī), *Ṭabaqāt al-Umam*, Najaf: al-Maktaba al-Ḥaydariyya (1967).

Ibn Sīnā, see Gohlman.

Ikhwān al-Ṣafā', *Rasā'il*, 4 vols, Beirut: Dār Ṣādir (1957).

—— See also Goodman, Shiloah.

Kopf, L., 'The Zoological Chapter of the *Kitāb al-Imtā' wal-Mu'ānasa* of Abū Ḥayyān al-Tauḥīdī (10th century)' (trans. from the Arabic and annotated), *Osiris*, vol. XII (1956), pp. 390–466.

Kraemer (trans.), '[Sijistānī's] On the Specific Perfection of the Human Species', see Kraemer, *Philosophy in the Renaissance of Islam: Abū Sulaymān al-Sijistānī and his Circle*, Leiden: E.J. Brill (1986).

Lunde, Paul and Stone, Caroline (trans. and eds), *The Meadows of Gold: The Abbasids*, by Mas'ūdī, London and New York: Kegan Paul International (1989).

Mahdi, Muhsin, see Fārābī, *Kitāb al-Ḥurūf.*

Mardrus, J.C. and Mathers, Powys (trans.) *The Book of the Thousand Nights and One Night*, 4 vols, London: Folio Society (1973, repr. from 1958 edn).

Mas'ūdī, *Kitāb al-Tanbīh wa 'l-Ishrāf*, Cairo: Dār al-Ṣāwī (1938).

—— *Murūj al-Dhahab*, 4 vols, Beirut: Dār al-Andalus (1966).

—— See also Lunde and Stone.

Miskawayh, *Kitāb Tajārib al-Umam*, 2 vols, ed. H.F. Amedroz, Baghdad: al-Muthannā (n.d.; repr. from Cairo: Sharikat al-Tamaddun al-Ṣinā'iyya edn of 1914–15).

Mutanabbī, *Dīwān al-Mutanabbī*, Beirut: Dār Ṣādir (1964).

—— See also Arberry.

Périer, Augustin (ed.), *Petits Traités Apologétiques de Yaḥyâ Ben 'Adî* (Arabic-French), Paris: J. Gabalda/Paul Geuthner (1920).

—— 'Un traité de Yaḥyâ ben 'Adî: Défense du dogme de la Trinité contre les objections d'al-Kindî', *Revue de l'Orient Chrétien*, no. 1, 3e Sér, t. II (= t. XXII) (1920–1), pp. 3–21.

Rescher, Nicholas and Shehadi, Fadlou (trans.), 'Yaḥyā ibn 'Adī's Treatise "On the Four Scientific Questions Regarding the Art of Logic"', *Journal of the History of Ideas*, vol. XXV (Oct.-Dec. 1964), pp. 572–8 (English trans. pp. 573–8).

Rosenthal, Franz, 'Abū Ḥayyān at-Tawḥīdī on Penmanship', in F. Rosenthal, *Four Essays on Art and Literature in Islam*, The L.A. Mayer Memorial Studies in Islamic Art and Archaeology, II, Leiden: E.J. Brill (1971), pp. 20–49.

Rowson, Everett Keith, 'Al-'Āmirī on the Afterlife: A Translation with Commentary of his *al-Amad 'alā l-Abad*', Ph.D. thesis, University of Yale (1982).

—— *A Muslim Philosopher on the Soul and its Fate: Al-'Āmirī's* Kitāb al-Amad 'alā l-Abad, American Oriental Series, 70, New Haven, Connecticut: American Oriental Society (1988). (Abbreviated as al-'Āmirī, *Kitāb al-Amad.*)

—— See also under Other Sources.

Shiloah, Amnon, *The Epistle on Music of the Ikhwan al-Safa (Baghdad, 10th century)*, Documentation and Studies: Publications of the Department of Musicology and the School of Jewish Studies, 3, Tel Aviv: Tel Aviv University (1978).

Sijistānī, Abū Sulaymān, *Fī 'l-Kamāl al-Khāṣṣ bi-Naw' al-Insān*, see Sijistānī, *Muntakhab*, ed. Badawī.

—— *Muntakhab Ṣiwān al-Ḥikma wa Thalāth Rasā'il*, ed. A.R. Badawī, Tehran: Intishārāt-i Bunyad-i Farhang-i Irān (1974).

—— *The Muntakhab Ṣiwān al-Ḥikmah of Abū Sulaimān as-Sijistānī*, Arabic text, introduction and indices, ed. D.M. Dunlop, Near and Middle East Monographs, IV, The Hague/Paris/New York: Mouton (1979).

—— See also Kraemer.

Ṭabarī, *Tārīkh al-Rusul wa 'l-Mulūk*, vol. 8, ed. Muḥammad Abū 'l-Faḍl Ibrāhīm, Dhakhā'ir al-'Arab, 30, Cairo: Dār al-Ma'ārif (1966).

—— See also Bosworth.

Takriti, Naji, *Yahya Ibn ʿAdi: A Critical Edition and Study of his Tahdhib al-Akhlaq*, Beirut/ Paris: Éditions Oueidat (1978).

Tawḥīdī, Abū Ḥayyān, *Akhlāq al-Wazīrayn*, ed. M. al-Ṭanjī, Damascus: al-Majmaʿ al-ʿIlmī al-ʿArabī (1965).

—— *Al-Baṣāʾir wa ʾl-Dhakhāʾir*, 4 vols, ed. Ibrāhīm Keilani (al-Kaylānī), Damascus: Maktabat Aṭlas/Maṭbaʿat al-Inshāʾ (1964).

—— *Kitāb al-Imtāʿ wa ʾl-Muʾānasa*, 3 pts, eds Aḥmad Amīn and Aḥmad al-Zayn, Beirut: al-Maktaba al-ʿAṣriyya (1953).

—— *Al-Muqābasāt*, ed. M.T. Ḥusayn, Baghdad: Maṭbaʿat al-Irshād (1970).

—— *Risāla fī ʿIlm al-Kitāba*, see Tawḥīdī, *Thalāth Rasāʾil*.

—— *Thalāth Rasāʾil li Abī Ḥayyān al-Tawḥīdī*, ed. Ibrāhīm al-Kaylānī, Damascus: al-Maʿhad al-Faransī bi-Dimashq li ʾl-Dirāsāt al-ʿArabiyya (1951).

—— See also Bergé, Kopf, Rosenthal.

Türker, Mubahat (ed.), 'Yaḥyā ibn ʿAdī ve Neşredilmemiş, bir Risalesi', *Ankara Üniversitesi Dil ve Tarih-Coğrafya Fakültesi Dergisi*, vol. XIV (1956), pp. 87–102 (contains Arabic text and Turkish trans.).

Walzer, Richard, *Al-Farabi on the Perfect State: Abū Naṣr al-Fārābī's Mabādiʾ Ārāʾ Ahl al-Madīna al-Fāḍila*, A rev. text with introd., trans. and commentary, Oxford: Clarendon Press (1985).

—— See also under Other Sources.

Yaḥyā b. ʿAdī, Maqāla fī ʾl-Tawḥīd li-Shaykh Yaḥyā b. ʿAdī 893–974/Le Traité de l'Unité de Yaḥyā ibn ʿAdī (893–974), ed. Khalil Samir, Patrimoine Arabe Chrétien no. 2, Jounieh: Librairie Saint-Paul/Rome: Pontificio Istituto Orientale (1980).

—— See also Périer (ed.), Rescher and Fadlou (trans.), Takriti, Türker (ed.).

Yāqūt, *Kitāb Irshād al-Arīb ilā Maʿrifat al-Maʿrūf bi-Muʿjam al-Udabāʾ*, vol. 5, 2nd edn. ed. D.S. Margoliouth, 'E.J.W. Gibb Memorial' Series, vol. 6, no. 5, London: Luzac (1929).

Zimmermann, F.W., *Al-Farabi's Commentary and Short Treatise on Aristotle's* De Interpretatione, trans. with introd. and notes, Classical and Medieval Logic Texts III, Oxford: published for the British Academy by Oxford University Press (1981).

Other Sources

Allan, D.J., *The Philosophy of Aristotle*, 2nd edn, Opus 37, London/Oxford/New York: Oxford University Press (1970).

Allard, Michel, 'Un Philosophe Théologien: Muḥammad b. Yūsuf al-ʿĀmirī, *Revue de l'Histoire des Religions*, vol. 187 (1975), pp. 57–69.

Anawati, G.-C. and Gardet, Louis, *Mystique Musulmane*, 3rd edn, Études Musulmanes VIII, Paris: Librairie Philosophique (1976).

Arberry, A.J., 'An Arabic Treatise on Politics', *Islamic Quarterly*, vol. 2, no. 1 (April 1955), pp. 9–22.

Aristotle, *Aristotle's* Metaphysics: *Books* Γ, Δ and Ε, trans. Christopher Kirwan, Clarendon Aristotle Series, Oxford: Clarendon Press (1971).

—— *The Politics*, ed. Stephen Everson, Cambridge Texts in the History of Political Thought, Cambridge: Cambridge University Press (1988).

Arkoun, Mohammed, 'Logocentrisme et Vérité Religieuse dans la Pensée Islamique d'après *al-I'lām bi-Manāqib al-Islām*, d'al-'Âmirī', *Studia Islamica*, vol. XXXV (1972)', pp. 5–51.

Arnaldez, Roger, 'Pensée et Langage dans la Philosophie de Fārābī (A Propos du *Kitāb al-Ḥurūf*)', *Studia Islamica*, vol. XLV (1977), pp. 57–65.

Ayer, A.J., *Language, Truth and Logic*, London: Gollancz (1936).

Badawī, 'Abd al-Raḥmān, *Histoire de la Philosophie en Islam*, 2 vols, Études de Philosophie Médiévale, 60, Paris: Librairie Philosophique J. Vrin (1972).

Barnes, Jonathan, *Aristotle*, Past Masters, Oxford/New York: Oxford University Press (1982).

Barthold, W. and Sourdel, D., art. 'Al-Barāmika', *EI*², vol. 1, pp. 1033–6.

Bergé, Marc, *Pour un Humanisme Vécu: Abū Ḥayyān al-Tawḥīdī*, Damascus: Institut Français de Damas (1979).

Bosworth, C.E., *The Islamic Dynasties*, Islamic Surveys 5, Edinburgh: Edinburgh University Press (1967).

—— *Sīstān under the Arabs, From the Islamic Conquest to the Rise of the Ṣaffārids* (30–250/651–864), ISMEO Centro Studi e Scavi Archeologici in Asia Reports and Memoirs vol. XI, Rome: ISMEO (1968).

—— See also Schacht and Bosworth.

Canard, M., art. 'Ḥamdānids', *EI*², vol. 3, pp. 126–31.

Dancy, Jonathan, *An Introduction to Contemporary Epistemology*, Oxford: Basil Blackwell (1985).

Daud, Wan Mohd Nor Wan, *The Concept of Knowledge in Islam and its Implications for Education in a Developing Country*, London: Mansell (1989).

Davidson, Herbert A., 'Alfarabi and Avicenna on the Active Intellect', *Viator*, vol. 3 (1972), pp. 109–78.

De Boer, T.J., *The History of Philosophy in Islam*, London: Luzac (1st edn 1903, repr. 1970).

Dunlop, D.M., *Arab Civilization to A.D. 1500*, Arab Background Series, London: Longman/Beirut: Librairie du Liban (1971).

—— art. 'Al-Balkhī', *EI*², vol. 1, p. 1003.

Encyclopaedia of Islam, New Edition, ed. H.A.R. Gibb *et al.*, 7 vols, cont., Leiden: E.J. Brill/London: Luzac (1960–).

Endress, Gerhard, *The Works of Yaḥyā ibn 'Adī: An Analytical Inventory*, Wiesbaden: Reichert (1977).

Everson, Stephen (ed.), *Epistemology*, Companions to Ancient Thought, 1, Cambridge: Cambridge University Press (1990).

—— See also Aristotle, *The Politics*.

Fakhry, Majid, *A History of Islamic Philosophy*, 2nd edn, London: Longman/ New York: Columbia University Press (1983).

Flew, Antony (ed.), *A Dictionary of Philosophy*, London: Pan Books and Macmillan (1979).

Gerhardt, Mia I., *The Art of Story-Telling: A Literary Study of The Thousand and One Nights*, Leiden: E.J. Brill (1963).

Goodman, Lenn Evan and Goodman, Madeleine J., 'Creation and Evolution: Another Round in an Ancient Struggle', *Zygon*, vol. 18, no. 1 (1983), pp. 3–43.

Guillaume, Alfred, *The Traditions of Islam: An Introduction to the Study of the Hadith Literature*, Khayats Oriental Reprint, 13, Beirut: Khayats (1966, repr. from O.U.P. edn of 1924).

Gutas, Dimitri, *Avicenna and the Aristotelian Tradition: Introduction to Reading Avicenna's Philosophical Works*, Islamic Philosophy and Theology Texts and Studies, IV, Leiden/New York/København/Köln: E.J. Brill (1988).

—— *Greek Wisdom Literature in Arabic Translation. A Study of the Graeco-Arabic Gnomologia*, American Oriental Series, 60, New Haven, Connecticut: American Oriental Society (1975).

Hamdani, Abbas, 'Abū Ḥayyān al-Tawḥīdī and the Brethren of Purity', *International Journal of Middle East Studies*, vol. 9 (1978), pp. 345–53.

—— 'The Arrangement of the *Rasā'il Ikhwān al-Ṣafā'* and the Problem of Interpolations, *Journal of Semitic Studies*, vol. XXIX, no. 1 (Spring 1984), pp. 97–110.

Hare, R.M., *Plato*, Past Masters, Oxford/New York: Oxford University Press (1982).

Holy Bible, trans. R. Knox, London: Burns & Oates/Macmillan (1960).

Horovitz, J., art. ''Abbāsa', EI^2, vol. 1, p. 14.

Hourani, George F., *Islamic Rationalism: The Ethics of 'Abd al-Jabbār*, Oxford: Clarendon Press (1971).

Hyman, Arthur and Walsh, James J. (eds), *Philosophy in the Middle Ages*, 2nd edn, Indianapolis: Hackett Publishing Company (1987).

Jadaane, Fehmi, 'La Philosophie de Sijistānī', *Studia Islamica*, vol. XXXIII (1971), pp. 67–95.

Jolivet, Jean, 'L'Intellect selon al-Fārābī: Quelques Remarques', *Bulletin d'Études Orientales*, vol. 29 (1977), pp. 251–9.

Juynboll, G.H.A., *Muslim Tradition: Studies in Chronology, Provenance and Authorship of Early* ḥadīth, Cambridge Studies in Islamic Civilization, Cambridge: Cambridge University Press (1983).

Kennedy, Hugh, *The Prophet and the Age of the Caliphates: The Islamic Near East from the Sixth to the Eleventh Century*, A History of the Near East, London/New York: Longman (1986).

Kirwan, see Aristotle.

Kraemer, Joel L., 'Abû Sulaymân As-Sijistânî: A Muslim Philosopher of the Tenth Century', Ph.D. thesis, University of Yale (1967). (Published in facsimile by University Microfilms, Inc., Michigan: Ann Arbor (1985).)

—— *Humanism in the Renaissance of Islam: The Cultural Revival during the Buyid Age*, Tel Aviv Studies in Islamic Culture and History Series, VII, Leiden: E.J. Brill (1986).

—— *Philosophy in the Renaissance of Islam: Abū Sulaymān al-Sijistānī and his Circle*, Tel Aviv Studies in Islamic Culture and History Series, VIII, Leiden: E.J. Brill (1986).

Leaman, Oliver, *An Introduction to Medieval Islamic Philosophy*, Cambridge: Cambridge University Press (1985).

Leavis, F.R., *The Great Tradition*, London: Chatto & Windus (1948).

Lewis, Bernard, *The Arabs in History*, 4th edn, Hutchinson University Library, London: Hutchinson (1968).

Liddell, H.G. and Scott, R., *An Intermediate Greek-English Lexicon, Founded upon the Seventh Edition of Liddell & Scott's Greek-English Lexicon*, Oxford: Clarendon Press (1968).

Madkour, Ibrahim, 'Al-Fārābī', see Sharif (ed.), *A History of Muslim Philosophy*, vol. 1, pp. 450–68.

—— *La Place d'al-Fârâbî dans l'École Philosophique Musulmane*, Librairie d'Amérique et d'Orient, Paris: Adrien-Maisonneuve (1934).

Mahjoub, Zadi, 'Abu Hayyan at-Tawhidi: Un Rationaliste Original', *Revue de l'Institut des Belles Lettres Arabes* (Tunis), vol. 27 (1964), pp. 317–44.

Marenbon, John, *Early Medieval Philosophy (480–1150): An Introduction*, London: Routledge & Kegan Paul (1983).

Marquet, Yves, *La Philosophie des Iḫwān al-Ṣafā'*, Algiers: Société Nationale d'Édition et de Diffusion (1973).

Meisami, Julie Scott, 'Mas'ūdī on Love and the Fall of the Barmakids', *Journal of the Royal Asiatic Society* 2 (1989), pp. 252–77.

Najjar, Fauzi M., 'Fārābī's Political Philosophy and Shī'ism', *Studia Islamica*, vol. XIV (1961), pp. 57–72.

Netton, Ian Richard, *Allāh Transcendent: Studies in the Structure and Semiotics of Islamic Philosophy, Theology and Cosmology*, Exeter Arabic and Islamic Series, London: Routledge (1989).

—— (ed.), *Arabia and the Gulf: From Traditional Society to Modern States*, London: Croom Helm (1986).

—— 'Arabia and the Pilgrim Paradigm of Ibn Baṭṭūṭa: A Braudelian Approach', in Netton (ed.) (1986), *Arabia and the Gulf*, pp. 29–42.

—— 'Basic Structures and Signs of Alienation in the *Riḥla* of Ibn Jubayr', *Journal of Arabic Literature*, vol. XXII, no. 1 (March 1991), pp. 21–37.

—— *Muslim Neoplatonists: An Introduction to the Thought of the Brethren of Purity (Ikhwān al-Ṣafā')*, London: Allen & Unwin (1982)/Edinburgh: Edinburgh University Press (1991) (Islamic Surveys 19).

—— 'Myth, Miracle and Magic in the *Riḥla* of Ibn Baṭṭūṭa', *Journal of Semitic Studies*, vol. XXIX, no. 1 (Spring 1984), pp. 131–40.

Nicholson, R.A., *A Literary History of the Arabs*, Cambridge: Cambridge University Press (1969).

O'Connor, D.J. and Carr, B., *Introduction to the Theory of Knowledge*, Brighton: Harvester Press (1982).

O'Leary, De Lacy, *Arabic Thought and its Place in History*, Trubner's Oriental Series, London: Routledge & Kegan Paul (1st edn 1922; rev. repr. edn 1968).

Omar, F., art. 'Hārūn al-Rashid', *EI*², vol. 3, pp. 232–4.

Parkinson, G.H.R. (ed.), *An Encyclopaedia of Philosophy*, London: Routledge (1988).

Pears, David, *What is Knowledge?*, Essays in Philosophy, London: Allen & Unwin (1972).

Peters, J.R.T.M., *God's Created Speech: A Study in the Speculative Theology of the Mu'tazilî Qâḍî l'Quḍât Abû l'Ḥasan 'Abd al-Jabbâr bn Aḥmad al-Hamaḏânî*, Leiden: E.J. Brill (1976).

Plato, *The Last Days of Socrates* (containing *Euthyphro, The Apology, Crito* and *Phaedo*), trans. Hugh Tredennick, Harmondsworth: Penguin (1971).

—— *The Republic*, trans. H.D.P. Lee, Harmondsworth: Penguin (repr. 1972).

—— *The Symposium*, trans. Walter Hamilton, Harmondsworth: Penguin (1972).

Plotinus, *Enneads*, 7 vols, trans. A.H. Armstrong, The Loeb Classical Library, London: Heinemann/Cambridge, Mass.: Harvard University Press (1966–88).

Proclus, *The Elements of Theology*, ed. E.R. Dodds. A rev. text with trans., introd. and commentary, Oxford: Clarendon Press (1933).

Qāḍī, Wadād, '*Kitāb Ṣiwān al-Ḥikma*: Structure, Composition, Authorship and Sources', *Der Islam*, vol. 58 (1981), pp. 87–124.

Rabe, Ahmad Abdulla, 'Muslim Philosophers' Classifications of the Sciences: al-Kindī, al-Fārābī, al-Ghazālī, Ibn Khaldūn', unpublished Ph.D. thesis, University of Harvard (1984).

Rescher, Nicholas, *Al-Fārābī: An Annotated Bibliography*, Pittsburgh: University of Pittsburgh Press (1962).

Robson, J., art. 'Al-Bukhārī, Muḥammad b. Ismā'īl, *EI*², vol. 1, pp. 1296–7.

—— art. 'Ḥadīth', *EI*², vol. 3, pp. 23–8.

Rosenthal, F., *The Classical Heritage in Islam*, trans. from German by Emile and Jenny Marmorstein, London: Routledge & Kegan Paul (1975).

—— *Four Essays on Art and Literature in Islam*, The L.A. Mayer Memorial Studies in Islamic Art and Archaeology, II, Leiden: E.J. Brill (1971).

—— *Knowledge Triumphant: The Concept of Knowledge in Medieval Islam*, Leiden: E.J. Brill (1970).

—— 'State and Religion According to Abû l'Ḥasan al-'Âmirî', *Islamic Quarterly*, vol. 3, no. 1 (1956), pp. 42–52.

Rowson, Everett Keith, art. 'Al-'Āmirī', *EI*² *Supp.*, Fascs 1–2, Leiden: E.J. Brill (1980), pp. 72–3.

—— See also under Arabic Sources.

Samir, Khalil, 'Le *Tahḏīb al-Aḫlāq* de Yaḥyā b. 'Adī (m. 974) attribué à Gāḥiẓ et à Ibn al-'Arabī', *Arabica*, vol. XXI (1974), pp. 111–38.

—— See also under Yaḥyā b. 'Adī in Arabic Sources.

Schacht, Joseph, art. 'Ḥiyal', *EI*², vol. 3, pp. 510–13.

—— and Bosworth, C.E. (eds), *The Legacy of Islam*, 2nd edn, Oxford: Clarendon Press (1974).

Shaban, M.A., *Islamic History: A New Interpretation, 2: A.D. 750–1055 (A.H. 132–448)*, Cambridge: Cambridge University Press (1976).

Sharif, M.M. (ed.), *A History of Muslim Philosophy*, 2 vols, Wiesbaden: Otto Harrassowitz (1963).

Sorell, T., 'The Analysis of Knowledge' in Parkinson (ed.), *An Encyclopaedia of Philosophy*, London: Routledge (1988), pp. 127–39.

Staniland, Hilary, *Universals*, New York: Doubleday (1972)/London: Macmillan (1973).

Stern, S.M., art. 'Abū Ḥayyān al-Tawḥīdī', *EI*², vol. 1, pp. 126–7.

—— art. 'Abū Sulaymān Muḥammad B. Ṭāhir B. Bahrām al-Sidjistānī', *EI*², vol. 1, pp. 151–2.

Vadet, Jean-Claude, 'Le Souvenir de l'Ancienne Perse chez le Philosophe Abū l-Ḥasan al-'Āmirī (m. 381 H.)', *Arabica*, vol. XI (1964), pp. 257–71.

—— *Une Défense Philosophique de la Sunna:* Les Manāqib al-Islām d'al-'Āmirī, REI-Hors Série 11, Paris: Librairie Orientaliste Paul Geuthner (1983).

Van Ess, Joseph, Review of Kraemer's *Philosophy in the Renaissance of Islam*, in *Journal of the Royal Asiatic Society* 1 (1988), pp. 174–5.

Walzer, Richard, art. 'Al-Fārābī, *EI*², vol. 2, pp. 778–81.

—— 'Al-Fārābī's Theory of Prophecy and Divination', in Walzer, *Greek into Arabic: Essays on Islamic Philosophy*, Oxford: Bruno Cassirer (1962), pp. 206–19.

—— *Greek into Arabic: Essays on Islamic Philosophy*, Oriental Studies, 1, Oxford: Bruno Cassirer (1962).

—— 'Some Aspects of Miskawaih's Tahdhīb al-Akhlāq', in Walzer, *Greek into Arabic*, pp. 220–35.

—— and Gibb, H.A.R., art. 'Akhlāḳ', *EI*², vol. 1, pp. 325–9.

—— See also under Arabic Sources.

Watt, W. Montgomery, *Islamic Philosophy and Theology: An Extended Survey*, 2nd edn, Edinburgh: Edinburgh University Press (1985).

Wehr, Hans, *A Dictionary of Modern Written Arabic*, 2nd printing, ed. J. Milton Cowan, Wiesbaden: Otto Harrassowitz (1966).
Wright, Owen, 'Music', in Schacht and Bosworth (eds), *The Legacy of Islam*, 2nd edn, Oxford: Clarendon Press (1974).

INDEX

In this Index the Arabic definite article 'al-' has been omitted from proper nouns at the *beginning* of an entry. 'B' and 'ibn' both appear as 'b' in the *middle* of a name.